The Soul of Real Estate:
Rethinking the World's
Greatest Profession

by

Ross R. Blaising
and Robbie R. Reese

Library of Congress Cataloging-in-Publication----------------------

The Soul of Real Estate: Rethinking the World's Greatest Profession by Ross R Blaising and Robbie R Reese.

ISBN 978-0-692-20557-0

Cover art by Lori Warner

The paper used in this publication meets the requirements of the American National Standard for Permanence of Paper for Publications and Documents in Libraries and Archives Z39.48-1992.

To the generations of developers to come,
whose passion and dedication to changing the world
may inspire us all.

Special thanks to:
Edith and Robert Blaising, Skip Beebe, Johnny Ladson,
Keith Mack, Brandon Ashkouti and Michael Presky

Scott,

To a good friend and fellow Idea Guy.

I hope you enjoy it!

Rob

Table of Contents

List of Figures viii

Introduction 1

Chapter 1: Forces at Work 4

    Suburbanization and Re-urbanization.......................... 8

    Suburbanization, Geography and Transportation 12

    Challenges and Opportunities 14

Chapter 2: The Problem 20

    An Example 23

    How Did We Get Here?.. 26

    The Effect of Capital on the Development Firm 31

    How Do We Fix It?... 37

Chapter 3: Definitions 38

    The Firm's Structure: Then and Now 39

    The Definition of Developer 45

    Definition of Success 52

Chapter 4: Goals, Values and Vision 56

    Culture... 58

    Mission.. 60

    Goals 61

    Values 62

    Beginning 66

    Vision.. 71

    The Vision Package 76

Chapter 5: The Litmus Test...79

    Beginning by Beginning 82

    The Litmus Test 86

    Financial Analysis...88

    Market Analysis 90

    Conclusion 108

Chapter 6: The 'M' Word...111

    Shifting Focus 114

    Challenges..117

    How Do We Do It? 122

    Mentorship 123

Chapter 7: Anatomy 136

    Dissection...140

    Connectivity 142

    TSORE Structure 149

    Conclusion 151

Chapter 8: Tectonics...153

    Focus 155

Chapter 9: Mad Men 158

    Purpose-Driven Marketing....................................160

    Development University 162

    Nut and Bolts 163

Chapter 10: The Laws of Attraction.............................167

    Positioning the Firm...170

    Changing Course...173

Chapter 11: Size Matters 177

    Capacity and Likelihood 178

Chapter 12: Old School, New School 210

    Admissions 212

        Phase 1. Data Collection 216

        Phase II. Vetting 220

        Phase III. Interviews 223

        Phase IV. Concluding the Process 224

        Other Issues. 226

Chapter 13: Onboarding 228

    PHASE I. The First Seven Days 230

    PHASE II. Days Eight Through Ninety 234

Chapter 14: Archetype I – The Leader 239

    The External Audience 252

    The Internal Audience 258

    Leadership Styles 261

Chapter 15: The Allegory of the String and the Bag 264

    Nuance 265

    The (un)Hero 267

    Harnessing Creativity and Limiting Chaos 273

Chapter 16: Archetype II – The Salesman 275

Chapter 17: Stability 287

    Critical Chaotic Issues 292

Chapter 18: "There Will Be Blood" 315

Appendix A: Vision Package 320

List of Figures

Figure 1. Manhattan: 150 Years of Growth 99

Figure 2. Getting Development Wrong: The View at Chastain
Lofts, Atlanta, Georgia.. 101

Figure 3. Vistas Along Boston's Newbury Street 105

Figure 4. Traditional Executive Organization.............................. 142

Figure 5. Typical Silo Structure 143

Figure 6. Typical Assembly Line Structure 145

Figure 7. Typical Matrix Structure... 147

Figure 8. Illustration of String Theory 270

Figure 9. Illustration of Bag Theory... 271

Figure 10. Typical Stability and Chaos within an Organization 290

Figure 11. Bonus Litmus Test... 302

Figure 12. Stability and Chaos within a TSORE Organization......314

Introduction

Over the past decades, real estate developers have come to rely on the ebb and flow of the business cycle. Since the 1960s, the peaks between these cycles have averaged between seven and ten years. So we unquestionably know that they are coming. During the upward pendulum swing of an economic cycle, we consistently invest. This occurs during the period of stable growth and through the inevitable debaucheristic overbuilding. Once the inevitable bubble bursts, we shift into the mode of holding on to as much of our investment portfolio as possible and attempt to avoid bankruptcy. Often we find ourselves battling demons that we ourselves created. Whether we were constructing too many projects, building and investing in risky locations, or cross-collateralizing our investments so that when one or two fail, they all fail; the problems that typically threaten our demise are our own greed and stupidity.

In addition, the product that the developer creates has become consistently more expensive, denser and more complex, and yet the structure of the firm has not metamorphosed itself to better contemplate the real world challenges that developers face. In fact, through some anti-Darwinian paradigm shift, the skills within our firms have devolved to the point that good, responsive, attractive and profitable buildings are more a product of chance than intelligent design. Whereas they were once tasked with placing a square peg in a square hole, the complexity of the responsibility hoist upon our current and future developers requires that they manufacture irregular pegs for a series of ever-changing shaped holes. Most of us are ill-prepared for this reality.

Our path is not yet set in stone. The opportunity remains ours to return the greatest of professions to its rightful magnificence. And so we real estate developers have two daunting tasks; first we must continue to evolve and make buildings, and second, we must reverse the downward trajectory of the profession of development. We must save development from the developers.

The following pages are intended to begin that conversation. Through part one of *The Soul of Real Estate* (TSORE) we will explore, opine and offer solutions to our most basic and existential dilemmas. We will suggest different values and provide a vision for the future. Part two will apply those premises toward a practical and methodical implementation. After all, we will surely fail if our solution doesn't seem achievable. We must dismantle the broken clock that is real estate development, and reengineer and reassemble its parts if we ever expect it to tell time again.

Because development firms differ in scale, region and product type, there is not a one-size-fits-all solution. Each of our organizations will be distinct. However, if the fundamental stability that we discuss is present in each of our organizations, the world of development (and consequently the world) will be a better place.

Our hope is that this discussion is one that we will have throughout our lives; first as students in school, later during the times when we are most beaten down and the profession feels bleakest, and again as we form the basis of our own firms. Our hope

2

is that we never again forgot who we are, why we do what we do, and how great it can be when we do it well. Our hope is that this conversation is just the beginning.

Chapter 1

Forces at Work

"We hold these truths to be self-evident" – Thomas Jefferson

The earth's population increases by approximately 75 million per year, of which only about 3.75% occurs in the United States. That 3.75%, however, accounts for roughly 2.8 million people. When we consider the 500,000 people who pass away each year, as well as a host of other factors, including immigration and increasing average life spans, etc., the annual growth rate in the U.S. is roughly 0.7%. While that rate of increase is relatively stable, each year the United States must accommodate the housing, shopping, eating, traveling, worshiping, congregating and recreational needs of an additional 2.2 million people.

Finding efficient and attractive ways of building these accommodations is one of the many jobs performed by the real estate developer every day. Our tasks are to create and recreate the built environment. Through the buildings, parks, roads and monuments that developers envision, we interpret and ultimately define the urban, suburban, exurban and rural experiences of the billions of people that inhabit the planet. With the landscape as our base, we sculpt and shape and morph our visions into a collage of spaces where society congregates to pursue its individual dreams.

One of the major tenets of our culture is the concept of the American Dream, which is basically the idea that each generation stands on the shoulders of its parents' achievements and accordingly experiences new and unique opportunities. In other words, our children will always face the prospect of a better life than we led. The fundamental belief in the United States is that *your* fate is in *your* hands to work and strive and achieve whatever goals to which you aspire. You are not guaranteed success, but you are promised the right to try.

A second major concept that is ingrained into the nation's psyche is American Exceptionalism. From its origins, this land was established as a refuge from religious, political and social tyranny and has represented a unique opportunity for individuals to determine their own fates. In his 1809 farewell presidential speech, Thomas Jefferson said: "Trusted with the destinies of this solitary republic of the world, the only monument of human rights, and the sole depository of the sacred fire of freedom and self-government, from hence it is to be lighted up in other regions of the earth, if other regions of the earth shall ever become susceptible of its benign influence."

The promise of freedom and liberty has proven so infectious that masses from every corner of the earth risk life and limb to reach our sacred shores. And it was this constant influx of new talent, labor and ideas that eventually stretched our geographic limits from the Atlantic Ocean to the Pacific. Along their way, people stopped and settled upon land where they could pursue their own dreams. For some, it was to own and operate their own farm; for others it was to congregate with those of like-minded beliefs; and for others still it was the opportunity to innovate and amass wealth. The American Dream combined with freedom, space and untapped natural resources has produced a consistently hopeful and resourceful people. It is that perspective that makes this "Land of Opportunity" into a laboratory of Exceptionalism.

The ways that our population has distributed itself over the past 300 years have fundamentally changed. Of course there have been constant natural ebbs and flows between urban and rural conditions; however, it was the Industrial Revolution and the opportunities for work and wealth it provided that placed our nation on its inextricable path toward increased density and urbanization. Unlike today, the majority of this activity was not concentrated in existing urban centers. Even during the early 20th century, much of the U.S. population still resided in the small towns that peppered our landscape.

A cursory review of the pop culture of the first four decades of the last century illustrates the romanticism of the small town. These medium-density organisms were the living, breathing hubs of industry, retaining both the character of the farm as well as the opportunities of community. They provided individuals with the opportunity to own small businesses (whether it was a restaurant, a store, a pharmacy, etc.), as well as allow access to amenities without the nuisances associated with big city life.

Naturally, large cities also continued to grow. In the mid-1900s, it was this growth, combined with the economic horsepower of returning GIs from World War II, the ease of owning an automobile, and the concept of the American Dream that fueled the trend of suburbanization. Millions of worker bees swarmed the cities in search of higher, more consistent pay. As some of them found success and economic comfort, their minds drifted back to that nostalgic American Dream in which the chance for achieving greater success than their parents prevailed. Rather than their tiny flats in Queens, thoughts drifted to a large yard, a white picket fence and a place where their children could run and play freely and safely. The suburb became the romantic ideal of small town virtues for city dwellers. And so, encircling the metropolis were established a series of communities which serviced the middle- and upper-middle classes.

The most interesting aspect of this phenomenon is that as large cities continued to grow, they swallowed up these initial suburbs. Each time this occurred, a new ring of suburbs was built, only to be digested and integrated into the fabric of the city. The result? The evolution of the American metropolis looks like the cross-section of a tree trunk, most obviously in landlocked cities.

Fast forwarding to today, the suburbanization trends that dominated the second half of the 20th century again have reversed. People who once flocked to more rural areas in search of the 1950s version of the American Dream now are gravitating *back* toward the city core in an attempt to shorten commutes and be in closer proximity with neighbors.

It is remarkable to consider that the American fantasy has shifted such that city life now seems more authentic. This has provided a substantial opportunity and challenge for the real estate developer.

Suburbanization and Re-urbanization

The urban core populations that decreased for decades while suburban and exurban populations grew at record paces are now trending in reverse. Not only have former suburbanites been incorporated into the city as its borders have expanded, but more and more people seek to return to the amenity-rich, high-density living as urban pioneering has become fashionable. Our "once upon a time" suburbs have grown, become bloated and now have their *own* suburbs, leaving most major markets with vast stretches of medium- and low-density urban fabric, aptly called suburban sprawl. (Once again, we recall the comparison of cities' expansion patterns to the growth rings of a tree trunk.) Out of this morass, new infrastructural and vehicular problems have arisen.

As major urban centers absorb their adjacent suburbs, the challenge of linking road grids and services, which were never designed to be linked at all, has resulted in a state of confusion and disunion. Municipalities struggle to rewrite and manage zoning codes while residents fight to retain their own neighborhood character. This should provide a spectacular opportunity for the real estate developer, as the new arteries will have undoubtedly required major redevelopment. Unfortunately, the conflict between neighborhood and municipality has often resulted in either stagnation of growth and progress, or only the most anemic development solutions. These ill-conceived compromises often lack longevity of success and will need to be redeveloped again, sooner rather than later.

Another challenge associated with suburbanization is unreasonable commuting distances. Regardless of our ability to get into our cars and travel slowly between neighborhood nodes on overcrowded streets, there remains an inherent reluctance among us to travel too far. Interestingly "too far" is actually a measure of time, rather than distance. In consistently greater numbers, suburbanites are refusing to relinquish two to three hours per day to time in a car simply to be able to afford a larger home and yard. After all, 2.5 hours per day, 5 days per week equals 650 hours, or 27 days per year of commuting. Effectively, that's sitting in traffic each second of the entire month of February, every year.

To increase the maneuverability between disjointed neighborhoods, city governments are forced to undergo the extremely expensive task of designating and fortifying new vehicular arteries. Part of the solution is to widen roads and add public transportation, and the other part of the solution is to re-entitle property with increased residential density and expanded retail uses. Within a capitalistic society like ours, a business model is quickly developed to address a need as it arises. In this case, the residential developer's opportunistic retail brethren quickly seized upon that emerging market need and adapted their business models to exploit it.

Recognizing the intrinsic link between the residential need for local retail conveniences, commercial developers responded by propagating main vehicular arteries with strip retail centers. The result has actually contributed to the logjam of traffic along our corridors. This was the first step in the retail evolution. By simply lining suburbia's more heavily used corridors with less dense retail uses, a demonic chain was created that perpetuated the post-WWII suburban sprawl that continues to plague our major cities. The length of the chain was limited only by one's tolerance for commuting to work. Only since the late 1990s has the criticism of suburban sprawl really begun to verifiably alter the way that zoning departments manage their strategic plans.

Earlier, we discussed the idea that many people moving back to major cities are doing so partly because of the feeling that it is a return to authenticity and vitality. In this regard, the suburban ideal of the American Dream has exposed itself as a fraud. This is not necessarily because suburbs are inherently bad, but rather because they often are erected too quickly, too artificially and with no true character. When a town or city grows over time, there is an intentionality and collective vision. But many of our recent suburbs will never possess such vitality, as they are often mere products of adjacent major developments. This generic, unnatural process is not capable of reflecting future resident's wishes or needs, nor is it designed to address potential problems that are solved relatively simply in cities whose growth occurs naturally. Instead, we are delivered a cookie-cutter town that can only pretend to appear authentic.

The approach to the land in suburbia is also very different. Instead of building logically and with deference to the natural environment, residential developers purchase large tracts of corn fields and woods, completely raze any natural features, disperse a series of homes clad in vinyl siding and cheap brick, and then replant anemic saplings and bushes around the lots. To add insult to injury, the neighborhoods are then given ridiculous names like "Williamsburg" (while reflecting none of its charm) or "The Shores at Beaver Creek." Never mind that creeks have banks not shores, and a beaver hasn't been spotted in the area in the last 50 years. These characterless suburban homes are simply boxes for living strewn across the landscape in an unconnected web of cul-de-sacs that typically lack any differentiating features. The saccharin quality of Suburbia has been recognized almost since its inception. Take Malvina Reynolds' song "Little Boxes," popularized during the 1960s by Pete Seeger and more recently used as the theme for the television show "Weeds," a show that mocks much of suburban life.

Little boxes on the hillside

Little boxes made of ticky tacky

Little boxes

Little boxes

Little boxes all the same

There's a green one and a pink one

And a blue one and a yellow one

And they're all made out of ticky tacky

And they all look just the same.

One last consideration is the tipping point at which suburbanization for the sake of the American Dream begins to displace the viability of the urban core. It usually results in greatly increased velocity of urban decay: higher crime rates, homelessness and a decreased tax base. The exodus of middle-class residents and their businesses leaves in its wake wastelands where prosperous cities once stood and declining neighborhoods whose remaining residents are too old or too poor to leave. Consequentially, this epidemic forces cities to face the prospect of shutting down entire school districts, vital city services or utilities, as was the case in Detroit, Michigan in the early 21st century.

Suburbanization, Geography and Transportation

If you look at the earliest U.S. metropolises, they share a single trait: most were built on waterways. Water was the preferred form of mercantile transport until the late 19th century, after which a web of railways was constructed to transport people and resources to previously unserviceable destinations throughout the country. The final nail in the coffin of inland water transport occurred in 1869 with the opening of the first transcontinental rail line, which connected the Atlantic and Pacific oceans. Railroads allowed for the establishment and growth of inland cities such as Denver, Salt Lake City, Atlanta, Phoenix, Dallas and Birmingham. In the mid-twentieth century, the creation of the Federal Highway Act formalized and funded a national push toward the interstate system that we know today, further reducing our ties to bodies of water. Finally, efficient air travel fully liberated the shipping economy from its once maritime shackles.

For decades, the growth model that we described above (in which suburbs were established, then gobbled up by the growing city, then a new series of suburbs established, etc.) progressed uninhibited – especially in America's younger cities that were not constrained by natural barriers. Cities established on oceans, lakes or in mountains settings contain greatly reduced areas of densely developable land. An island like Manhattan is the ultimate example of this phenomenon, as it is constrained in all directions. If we return to the concept that, at least in terms of suburban expansion, "too far" is a measure of time rather than distance, it is clear that our oldest cities would be at a great disadvantage if they were adjacent to a major body of water. These cities' solutions for continued growth would be less suburban expansion combined with greatly increased density.

The second critical effect that natural impediments have on development is the price of land. Returning to our capitalistic principles, it is not difficult to surmise that the more people moving into any urban situation that is directionally limited in its growth will result in competition for the existing, limited space. The consequence of competition is always a change in value. This is where density enters the equation. As land prices inflate, developers require more density and diversity of uses and revenue streams to support the additional cost.

Considering all this, the abundance of unconstrained land in most or all directions has provided younger inland cities with the inexpensive canvas on which our suburban sprawl has been painted. For inhabitants, particularly those with lower skill levels and lower pay, living in expensive, high density cities, the prospect of a cleaner, cheaper life elsewhere has gradually become more attractive and sometimes even necessary provided that the person's skill-set is transferable to the new location. New, inexpensive venues are also attractive to large manufacturing companies, where cheaper living expenses equals cheaper labor equals greater profits, and so on. After all, Nike doesn't manufacture its shoes in the developing economies of Asia because of their superior native craftsmanship. All of this contributes to suburbanization in America and around the globe.

Challenges and Opportunities

Both suburbanization and re-urbanization face inherent challenges and opportunities. From the suburbanization perspective there are two primary challenges:

1. How to make a series of roads and amenities (i.e., public transportation, waste management services, etc.) which were never intended to work together, somehow make efficient, cohesive sense.

2. How to mitigate the challenge of "too far" in regard to commuting.

From the re-urbanization perspective, a third challenge arises:

3. How to incorporate and make affordable the reintroduction of greater numbers of residents and amenities into underutilized areas in need of revitalization.

The first two challenges are nothing new. Cities have struggled with each of these since the 1950s. As regards the first issue, and mentioned earlier, the solution for many years for fortifying designated new arteries was to widen roads where possible and allow commercial uses along them. This solution served two purposes:

1. It helped municipalities to encourage the public to move in preordained patterns. The new retail and commercial uses gave the commuter reasons to use those preferred roads.

2. The new retail uses generated additional revenue. This increased tax base continued to fund infrastructural expansion activity. The development opportunities perpetuated the cycle that would become known as "suburban sprawl."

The real problems associated with this solution were not immediately evident. It was not until the roads were sufficiently lined with independent, single-tenant buildings (each of which required its own autonomic ingress and egress) that we could see that the increased tax base was also increasing vehicular congestion and commute times. From an aesthetic perspective, these miles of slow moving retail arteries generally become some of the biggest eyesores in our cities.

The cycle is one in which commuters spend increasing amounts of time moving farther and slower in increasingly ugly environments. It begs the question: "For what?" So we can stop and buy a hamburger or a coffee every 30 seconds? The irony is that our collective choice to "stop-and-grab" for the sake of sustaining us during our long commutes actually slows the arteries, which only reinforces and perpetuates our need to "stop-and-grab" again. It's a repulsive cycle.

As commute times reached their tipping points, a new trend emerged. Cities began to decentralize into what became known as "nodal cities." The nodal city is not a foreign concept; most of us live in them. They are simply cities that contain multiple (and generally peripherally clustered) business cores. Each of these new nodes enables its surrounding suburbs to return to reasonable commutes. Sadly, two of the unintended consequences of the nodal urbanity are that it further enables suburbanization and often divests the original city core of necessary financial resources, which eventually leads to urban decay.

Atlanta, Georgia is a prime example. If you were to visit Atlanta for the first time without a local guide, you would go to the city's downtown area to seek out the nightlife and restaurants and energy you would expect of a city of six million people. After wandering around aimlessly for 30 or 40 minutes, you'd return to your hotel and frustratingly say: "What an abomination! I can't see why anyone would want to live here."

What you wouldn't realize is that you were two miles from Midtown, which has been revitalized throughout the 1990s and early 2000s and has a terrific energy. You would be six miles from Buckhead, a neighborhood where much of the city life is concentrated. Buckhead was once a distant suburb of Atlanta where the city's most affluent kept their country homes and farms. Now, it's a 10-minute commute from downtown. Even *with* this knowledge, you would likely miss the various commercial and employment centers (nodes) of Cumberland, Perimeter, Vinings, Alpharetta and Decatur. Each of these is its own partially self-sufficient economic center. As the surrounding suburban landscape has grown and become increasingly dense, these economic centers have grown and become links in the chain described earlier. The result is that they can now support yet another layer of suburbia yet to be created, even more distant from the city's center.

Atlanta has seven centers – that's seven downtowns – and one gigantic identity crisis. While some suburbs are better than others, from a macro-perspective the "good" suburbs are rare enough that they appear as merely islands of traditional urban planning in a vast sea of banality. Once again, the homogeneity of the cul-de-sac lifestyle that is the suburban experience is a direct result of the unrestrained capitalistic development of farmland that is unencumbered by planning and zoning regulations. As mentioned, the song "Little Boxes" has aptly captured the funhouse mirror distortion of the American Dream. Gertrude Stein's description of Oakland, California also summed it up perfectly when she said, "There's no 'there' there."

The third challenge we face is re-urbanizing the now decaying urban core whose decline was partially caused by the nodalization of the city. Because the cores have deteriorated economically, it is now affordable to purchase and redevelop or repurpose the property. These sections of town often contain older buildings with rich details or are rife with abandoned factories or warehouses. It may be that crime has increased with the decay and that the city is incentivizing developers to swoop in and intervene.

Areas like this evoke a spirit of nostalgia, which is a strong part of the American Dream. There is much romance associated with re-gentrification that lies in both the realms of evoking simpler times gone by and also with making the world a better, more usable place. Combine this with the frustration of a long daily commute and you have the ingredients for a re-urbanization revolution. Sometimes it's more appealing to paint on a dirty canvas than a pristine one.

One of the greatest challenges with redevelopment derives from the fact that it is almost always much more expensive. Beginning with the land, which may have a building on it that needs to be refurbished or demolished, there are additional expenses. Also, if the site is not in complete catastrophic decay, then it likely contains some sort of commercial use. Even a poorly performing, income-producing use is still exponentially more expensive than raw land. And, of course, depending on the site and surrounding conditions, there may be additional construction costs associated with building in an urban location.

The solution to this is very simple and straightforward: the property will have to support much greater income in order to make sense. In almost every case, greater income translates to increased density. That density may come from single or multiple uses (residential rental, for-sale residential, office, hotel or retail), which is referred to as mixed-use.

Mixed-use is not a new typology by any means; however, it is one that is becoming increasingly popular and subsequently complex. The advantage to the city is that it forces developers to think about and actively create a viable streetscape that hopefully encourages activity, vibrancy and commerce, both day and night. To the developer it's an opportunity to diversify his risk. Whether the intention is simply to incorporate multiple revenue streams in an attempt to hedge against inevitable market fluctuations, or to sell off the varied components in order to lower the basis in the land, mixed-use can be an ideal solution.

But seemingly ideal solutions aren't always that. As we'll see, the increased capital requirements and complexity associated with mixed-use considerably raises the developer's stakes.

Chapter 2

The Problem

"Everybody needs money. That's why they call it money."
– Mickey Bergman, Heist

The mixed-use typology has delivered multiple opportunities to our urban cores and nodes. Although it's a solution typically born from the necessity to compensate for the increased cost of re-development projects, mixed-use propagation has many positive effects on the city. It promotes walkable neighborhoods by integrating living, working and entertainment spaces. In many of the best cases, the resulting product reflects traditional neighborhood design, albeit at much greater densities and scale. It promotes the American Dream by offering spaces for small entrepreneurs to pursue their individual goals. Additionally, well-planned mixed-use neighborhoods promote a vibrant backdrop for the exchange of ideas, commerce and calories. All of these pursuits can benefit the lives of all of the cities' inhabitants.

However, for a city to seize this energy and extract its potential, the developers who take on the investment and rebuilding *must* be expert and fully focused on their tasks. Mixed-use development is considerably more complicated than traditional, stand-alone building development and requires a more dexterous approach to building. We can chalk much of this complexity up to Project Sequencing, Relationships and Contractual Continuity.

1. *Project Sequencing.* The commercial multi-family and the commercial office and retail industries have very different approaches to commencing and funding a project. Every apartment development is a spec property, which the owners can't start leasing until they are a couple of years into the investment (greater risk). From a retail perspective, most developers don't begin spending real money until they have at least a Letter Of Intent (LOI) in place (lesser risk). The result is often that the multi-family developer has a significant waiting period after he's committed to the deal, while the retail partner locks down the lead tenants. The distinction of one partner having his primary tenants identified and the other having no tenants at all results in the forced marriage of at least two typologies with very different risk profiles.

2. *Relationships.* Ask any developer and he'll tell you that real estate development is a "relationship business." Another challenge of mixed-use development is that most multi-family developers lack the retail relationship expertise and vice versa. It is not uncommon for developers to undertake a major mixed-use development with specialists in whichever skill they lack. Because equity investors are similarly stratified and often focus their energies on specific product types, there is symmetry between how both capital and implementation must syndicate its expertise.

3. *Contractual Continuity.* The mixed-use typology also requires exponentially more complex legal constructs. From a

partnership perspective, are the partners in the JV equally yoked together? Do the various parties share in the ownership of all parts of the project? If there are multiple equity partners, how are risks segregated? And then there are the legal considerations for ongoing operations of the property. For instance, if the building is comprised of multi-family over retail, who is responsible if a residential tenant drops a hammer off a balcony onto an exposed retail roof and damages it? This and dozens of other concerns must be contemplated in order to establish a reasonable operating platform for design and construction, as well as ongoing operations and the eventual disposition.

So for a mixed-use vision to ever come to fruition, the land must be available and the city governance must be supportive of greatly increasing the density such that it is attractive to developers. A development team must be formed which can create and implement a vision that is attractive to the inhabitants, to investors for equity and debt, and also to retail tenants. An intricate legal framework must be created. Retailers must commit. And finally, significant risk must be taken with the belief that compelling profits will be made.

All of these are very solvable issues, but inarguably it is a much more complex proposition than purchasing a cornfield and sprinkling it with single-family homes. In order to address this added complexity, the skills of the developer must be broader, greater and more precise than at any time in our professions' history.

Unfortunately, at a time when the demands of an increasingly intricate and capital-intensive product type require equally increasing expertise and understanding, the developer's skills are becoming increasingly less sophisticated. The results of the widening gap between product requirements and the developer's ability to satisfy them is already evident.

An Example

How many times have you passed a new apartment complex with 8,000 to 15,000 square feet of retail space, and you only see a nail salon and a virtually empty Chinese restaurant and three or four vacant storefronts? Looking at the building and neighborhood it is painfully clear to you that 'Retail makes no sense as a part of this property.' Or perhaps the *location* is decent for retail use, but the space doesn't work because the ingress and egress is awkward, or maybe the parking segregation isn't well executed. As you examine it, you immediately know that a sophisticated retailer will never lease this space. If someone ever *does* lease or purchase the building, it will simply be the beginning of a perpetual cycle of failing short-term neighborhood investments, causing heartache for the tenant and for the building's owner, an equally undesirable cycle of chasing rent payments, evicting tenants, decreasing rents, added tenant improvement concessions and eventually, releasing the space. How many times have you seen potentially good projects fail for the wrong reasons? How many times have you seen developers steal defeat from the jaws of victory?

Of course, if the developer were asked about this abomination, he would talk about the ridiculous zoning category that was necessary to get the density required to justify the land price. He would go on to bemusedly explain that he suspected that the retail would never work, had explained it repeatedly to the city or county, and in the end it was easier to just build the space because he found a way to make the project profitable despite the middling retail performance. Then, with a little laugh he even let you in on a little secret: the retail couldn't have worked anyway because his bonehead development manager only made the space 55-feet deep because he didn't really understand the critical dimensions of the retail development anyway. Don't worry; he'll get it right next time.

This works out well: the developer earned his fee and paid his employees, received a portion of the promoted interest in the deal and bought a new Ferrari; the equity partners in New York made their profits; the bank was paid back; the asset was sold to an insurance conglomerate in Connecticut; and everyone is waiting for him to do it again.

This is simply not the way to do business. Here's the problem: it's not just one bad developer who is constructing poorly-programmed buildings because he can figure out how to make the numbers work; there are 10 or 20 more just like him. So, that 10,000 square feet of unusable space is actually 100,000 (or 200,000) square feet – per year, per city.

So what are the results of this development travesty?

First, neighborhood associations see the empty space and say, "These developers don't know what they're doing. There's already plenty of space out there to be rented. Why do I want to give this guy permission to build something that I don't want and my community doesn't need?" And so we propose, they oppose, and the city's final verdict is: "not in my back yard."

Next, our county commissioners (or other elected officials), who may actually understand the problems from both the developer's and the community's perspective, tend to support their constituents as they interact with local municipalities because their primary belief is that what is best for the community is that they get reelected.

Third, local municipalities misdiagnose the simple problems that actually lie within their zoning codes and ignore fixing the issues, or better yet enact a building moratorium to "study" the situation. So we sit and wait, and we all watch as these vacant spaces become ugly and neglected or the developers spend years trying to convert the non-performing retail to some other potential use. During this moratorium period, local taxes are suppressed as the poorly-situated retail spaces decay and no new quality product is produced. This causes a reduced tax base, resulting in a corresponding reduction in local investments in infrastructure. The degrading infrastructure further entrenches the neighborhood's position that the area is not equipped for new development, even if they wanted it.

Eventually, and somewhat miraculously, the cycle is broken because the municipality recognizes that it must begin to grow again, or go bankrupt. The moratorium is lifted and developers flock to invest in the area. The problem is that the abundance of vacant and decaying retail has depressed local rents such that the developers' margins are thinner, and many deals either barely work or don't financially work at all. The perceived higher risks – a result of the increased vacancy rates and lower rents – causes the developer's equity and debt to become less abundant and more expensive, further depressing his profit margin and making the development less attractive to execute. The ultimate result is that the buildings of higher density, integrated mixed-use projects that support neighborhood entrepreneurship are less feasible.

How Did We Get Here?

In the previous chapter, we discussed at length the many societal, intellectual and technological motivations that have shaped our cities and suburbs. We have addressed the forces that have recently moved our product toward greater scale and complexity. How then is it possible that as the demands upon the developer have so obviously increased, our acumen has so greatly decreased?

It may be difficult to hear, but for most of the industry, the corporate structure, career path and hiring practices that created us are outdated and flawed. While each of us brings our slightly different experiences, insights and prejudices to the table, one common factor is that as a community, we continue to create uglier and less responsive buildings,[1] simply because the land entitlements are in place and we are able to raise the necessary capital to execute the project.

Many developers have forgotten that, as developers, we are servants to the community's needs. We have lost sight of the fact that as real estate developers, we choose to change the world and, as such, have a responsibility to make the best decisions possible on a myriad of levels: typology, appropriateness, density, aesthetics and more. This responsibility extends to projects of all types and at every price-point. What our organizations often lack are the skills necessary to identify and make the best decisions.

Take a look at your current organization and each that you have worked in previously. Have these companies been structured to address all of the factors that affect the success of their development projects – or just the financial ones? Did your employees or co-workers have the skills necessary to evaluate and perform successfully without the principal's oversight? Were these companies built to encourage innovation and train future generations without constant guidance? If the answer to most of these questions is no, these firms were examples of the breakdown in the system. The good news is that there is a solution.

---

[1] For the authors' intents and purposes, 'less responsive' means less comprehensively usable and adaptable for our communities' current and future uses. It does not necessarily mean less aesthetically pleasing or energy efficient (although that may also be the case).

The source of many of our industry's problems resides in the DNA of the typical development organization, in its fundamental structure and focus. In short, our companies are not set-up to address the increasingly complex financial, urbanistic, legal and aesthetic issues that we and the future generations of developers that we are training will ultimately face.

Think about it: the genesis of the modern, scalable multi-family industry as we know it was the confluence of robust capital structures with a semi-dense, yet relatively simple construction typology that we called "garden style." The industry's large-scale reproducibility relied on multiple external factors: the suburbanization of our cities, inexpensive land, decreasing fuel costs, relatively unsophisticated zoning regulations, and access to "cheap" money. The shift in business model from smaller, localized developers to the large, national organizations that pump out 3,000 or more dwelling units annually was actually just an application of an established business model to a new product type. It was not a revolution. In the same way that Henry Ford applied the mass production business model adapted from Civil War firearms manufacturers to the automobile industry, our multi-family forefathers did the same with the post WWII single-family development business model.

The brilliance of the great early-modern multi-family developers, the Trammell Crow's, Mack Pogue's, Jerry Speyer's of this country, was timing. There was a great shift from home ownership to renting during the 1970s, as war veterans were coming home from Vietnam and children of the late 1950s were coming of age. In fact, the national apartment vacancy rate dropped below five percent (from historically typical rates then above eight percent) during the period. Many factors including the oil embargo, weak leadership at the Federal Reserve Board, and misguided social policy in the executive branch led to double-digit inflation in which the real price of goods tripled, making home ownership an unwieldy proposition. Down payment requirements in excess of 30 percent and interest rate percentages in the high-teens all but excluded most young people as first time homebuyers. This spiked the need for rental product of which only a handful of developers took advantage on any scale.

Once the recession showed signs of easing and the economy began to stabilize (and most importantly, the prime interest rates and price of gasoline dropped), consumers began another cycle of suburbanization, seeking more land and a simpler lifestyle. A few established apartment developers were poised to meet the growing preference for medium density rental units in a park-like setting (i.e., "garden style"). Previously, we discussed the American Dream of owning a home in the suburbs; however, economic realities provided a new opportunity for an application of that suburban dream. Garden-style apartments became the vehicles intended to provide the opportunity for those who had not yet attained the financial wherewithal necessary to own their own home.

The quantity of product began to explode with direct correlation to greater access to large sums of less expensive capital. A major differentiator between this growth explosion and the previous major expansions at the turn of the century and after WWII was that developers were shifting from using their own capital as their primary equity source to using external "institutional" capital from insurance companies and equity funds. The importance of this liquidity shift was both a much larger capacity to execute development projects and a disassociation of a sense of ownership felt by the developer. In other words, by decreasing the amount of a developer's personal capital that was at risk, the developer in turn was incented to take on more and sometimes riskier developments. Great fortunes were made by the developers who were able to exploit this economic lifecycle, which continued through the end of the 1980s.

From an overall quality-of-product standpoint, however, there was at best only anemic progress, as buildings went up rapidly without incorporating any major evolution into the model. Looking back to the apartment complexes constructed in the 1970s and 1980s, there were no significant construction or urbanistic differentiators from a 1940s army barracks. Aesthetically, there were various post-modern façade applications and roof treatments (three-story buildings with mansard roofs or tudor-esque appliqués), but underneath, the bones were exactly the same. The ingredients were simple and established and the recipe was reproducible enough that those who learned it could start their own firms and bake the very same cake almost anywhere in the country, needing only to raise the capital. Out of this opportunity came a wave of multi-family developers that have since spread across the landscape.

The Effect of Capital on the Development Firm

We know that people respond to incentives. Whether the rewards are praise or financial compensation or any number of other potential prizes, we all seek recognition. Our parents, our churches and our employers all have used their own incentives to encourage us to adopt specific behaviors. When the scale of those incentives is aligned with the intended goals, great things can happen. However, when those incentives are either out of scale or misaligned, then there is potential for very unintended consequences. And of course, what is true for us as individuals is also true for corporations.

There are countless anecdotes about the misalignment of incentives in corporate America. One of the authors' favorites is about Texas billionaire Ross Perot (founder of EDS) when he was a salesman at International Business Machines. Within IBM in the early 1960s, there was an idea about the maximum a salesman should earn each year. To ensure that a salesman would not exceed that annual amount, IBM instituted a commission cap. Because young Perot had been a hard-working and resourceful salesman over the years, he had established a great book of business. Beginning on January 1, 1962 Perot began working to meet his annual sales goals. In February of that year he reached his quota and took the next 10 months off, during which time he created Electronic Data Systems, a company he later sold to GM for $2.5 billion.

In this particular case, the predetermination of the value of a salesman and the subsequent decision to cap their compensation led to IBM equally capping their own profitability (at least within

Perot's business unit). This was an unintended and detrimental consequence due to misaligned incentives. The same phenomenon has occurred within the profession of real estate development.

There was a time decades ago when the real estate developer was larger than life. He was a heroic character who was a master of all trades. From banking to politics to construction to sales, the real estate developer was a visionary who bent the land to his will. He was the master artist of the landscape; he was the Raphael, the Donatello, the Michelangelo (and that other Teenage Mutant Ninja Turtle as well). But something changed the equation, which slowly and subtly altered the entire profession. That something was the influx of institutional capital.

Before we go too far down the path of explaining the effects of capital on the real estate development industry, let us first state unequivocally that the authors are fans of capital. We respect and appreciate the need for great sums that only institutional investment can deliver.

As certain development firms recognized the mass-production opportunities that were becoming apparent due to home ownership constraints of the 1970s as well as cheap land available during that suburban pioneering era, they quickly realized that of all of their potential limitations, the greatest and most critical was money. After all, construction typologies remained simple. Land was plentiful. The political climate and business cycles remained somewhat stable and predictable. Developers with regional or national aspirations recognized that the only gating factor to fulfilling their visions was their access to capital. They were incentivized to become adept at raising money.

The realization that the lifeblood of any scalable development enterprise was large sums of capital had two primary effects on the development industry. The first was much less insidious than the second.

1. A new typology was created; *the merchant developer (or merchant builder)*. Because merchant building is so common to us today, it is difficult to imagine a time when it did not dominate the industry. Merchant development actually began in the late 1940s by a select number of single-family developers who were providing low-cost housing for returning GIs. It was these early merchant builders who actually facilitated much of the middle and working class parts of suburbia that we have discussed. And it wasn't until much later that the model was applied to multi-family.

   By today's standards, the merchant developer is simply a company that builds commercial buildings with the intent to sell them. Note the addition of the word "commercial." This is significant because whether it's a Wal-Mart or a 300-unit apartment complex, incorporating commercial buildings is a huge shift in scale from this category's forefathers who built single-family homes with the intention of selling to individuals. And it is within this shift in scale that the real danger lies.

Because large-scale projects are so capital-intensive, the logical equity partner shifted from being a group of doctors from the country club to large insurance companies and private equity firms. It is no coincidence that these new equity sources are also the ideal end-owners of the asset that is being developed. In many cases, this new relationship has caused a passive shift from the heroic developer described above, who used his capital partners to facilitate his vision and dreams, to the lackey developer who creates product at the direction of the equity source for the enrichment of his shareholders.

The obvious challenge with this shift is one of motivation. Shareholders don't care about the quality of the product or the appropriateness of the site or the effect on the city; they care simply about the return on their investment. And while we'll grant you that ROI is a critical aspect of any investment, the danger lies in the situation where profit becomes the sole goal. Real estate is not a stock.

The merchant development model encourages the developer to disassociate himself from making prudent decisions for neighborhoods, for cities and for society as a whole. Because he is acting at the behest of his equity partner to get as much product in the market as possible, and because the equity partner has facilitated the developer in decreasing his personal at risk investment, the developer is no longer incentivized to make good long-term decisions. This leads to the situations described in the example at the beginning of the chapter. And it is this new misalignment of goals and risk, which has ultimately undermined the integrity of the profession, leaving us in our current situation.

2. One of the unintended consequences of the profession's shift to a merchant development model is that it has altered the way in which modern development firms structure themselves. Consider again the point made at the beginning of this section regarding the influence of incentives on our growth. The developer has for decades now worked under the understanding that the singular precious resource for his firm is its access to capital. Unquestionably, this knowledge has had an effect on the way that he fosters and protects his strategic relationship with his equity partner, the way that he values the appropriateness and viability of a potential building site, as well as how he structures his firm.

Each of these effects has played a part in the long-term decay of our industry. The first issue, "the strategic relationship," has shifted the power structure between the developer and capital such that the developer no longer controls the development process. Nor is the relationship one of equals. Under our current system, many developers have become so accustomed to suckling the teats of capital that they have bred out their pioneering, visionary underpinnings. They have become domesticated.

The second issue, "the ability to evaluate a potential project," has become less astute. Like any faculty or ability that is ignored, its sensitivity becomes retarded and numb. Developers have outsourced their expertise in urbanism and site assembly to focus on banking. What was once an expert developer is now a project manager and a conglomeration of consultants. Only pages ago, we said, "It may be difficult to hear, but for most of the industry, the corporate structure, career path and hiring practices that created us are outdated and flawed." Younger developers, those under 45, may not have had the opportunity to work for a truly heroic developer. And if you have never witnessed the power and acumen of a man whose skills and sensibilities are sharp and clean and focused on the task of good building (not only for the investors, but for the community), then it is difficult to blame them for not seeking that which is greater than the individual, or more satisfying than just the dollars.

The third issue, "the structure of the firm," is perhaps the greatest failure of modern development. By focusing our efforts on satisfying the whims of bankers rather than molding their skills to fit our needs, the development firm has grown to occupy a non-descript interstitial space. We are neither here nor there, neither builder nor banker. This situation is most evident at the entrance into the profession, where young would-be developers are typically liberated from consultancies, accounting firms and investment banks. For most, the skill that gains entrance into the hallowed halls of our industry is an understanding of cash flows and spreadsheets.

Regardless of the pontifications on our websites, we can more honestly see what a firm values by the skills that gain our admission into it. Increasingly, that skill is one that is far removed from those that determine our long-term success as developers. At the same time, the training and education of the developer is further directed to financial pursuits. With each successive generation we produce a group of developers who are less comprehensively trained and therefore less likely to be able to make consistently good decisions.

How Do We Fix It?

By marrying an understanding of the external forces that provide the constraints and opportunities that the developer faces each day with an etymology of the profession's past and present, we can hopefully chart a more purposeful path to the future. Our goal is to restore our profession's greatness such that we are again equipped to meet the needs of our increasingly complex building typologies. We must reverse our cities' and suburbs' trend toward banality and ugliness. And we must do so in a way that is self-perpetuating.

This task is overwhelming and seems perhaps too large for the individual firm. We cannot reverse the course of our industry as any single firm, but we can change the trajectory of the profession. The following chapters are intended to bind us to that goal with some commonality. We are changing the language so that we can have a new conversation – or rather an old one.

Chapter 3

Definitions

"Not every boy thrown to the wolves becomes a hero."
– John Barth

A primary theme of *The Soul of Real Estate* is that fundamental aspects of real estate development are broken and must be addressed to safeguard the profession's long-term viability. Our first two chapters introduced and discussed the forces at work from a macro perspective. We introduced the central maxim, "With each successive generation, we produce a group of developers who are less comprehensively trained and therefore less likely to be able to make consistently good decisions." In order to have a chance at reversing the Munchausian spiral in which our profession is currently cycling, we need to be able to address the situation at a molecular level.

One of the topics discussed in the last chapter was that the developers' reliance on institutional capital and the emergence of the merchant developer has negatively altered the structure of the development firm. This relationship has also skewed the way developers view their roles within the community. Most destructively, it has also shifted their views of what it means to be successful. These changes that we refer to were neither overt, nor intentional. And because they have occurred over decades, they have been virtually imperceptible. If we consider chapters 1 and 2 to be a forensic accounting of how we have gotten to this place in time, only a more Darwinian approach will allow us forecast the steps necessary to restore our profession's future.

Of the three topics to be discussed in this chapter – the altered structure of the development firm, the changed definition of the developer, and the shifted definition of success – the first and most basic task is understanding the firm in its current form and how that has evolved over decades. This establishes our latitude and longitude.

The Firm's Structure: Then and Now

It is somewhat difficult to classify the real estate development firm as failing when it both clearly remains in business and often provides large profits for its principals and partners. That said, this is exactly the point that we are going to make. Just as a bridge's structural failure does not necessarily mean it collapses, structural failure in the development firm does not mean that it ceases to exist. Failure is actually the condition under which the firm is no longer able to adequately and consistently manage all its responsibilities to its partners, its community and its own values. Under our current configuration, most firms are designed simply to enrich its partners, ignore or less villainously, not consider, its community and the *value* of values has degenerated into nonsensical MBA speak.

The result of this influence is an altered structure of the development firm, which has consequently produced a new definition of 'developer.' Revising both of these definitions is a significant step in returning our efforts to something greater than numbers in an Excel workbook.

The premise of our argument is that because the developer has been able reduce his risk to virtually nothing through implementation of the merchant model, the concern for the long-term health and usability of a project has also diminished. It will, after all, be leased-up, then sold to a major insurance company, REIT or opportunity fund. The long-term consequences of questionable decisions are no longer the developer's problem, especially if the issues are not immediately glaringly apparent. And if the developer is not concerned with the long-term viability of their buildings, certainly they are not concerned with the betterment of the cities in which the buildings reside. So, what this lack of interest in viewing the investment as an ongoing concern means two things are likely to occur:

1. The developer no longer hires senior developers with an A-Z skill-sets and instead looks chiefly for financial acumen.

2. The developer no longer trains his younger employees to have or even *respect* the full scope of the development process.

Such is the devolution of the industry. Within only a couple of generations (roughly seven to ten year increments), the development firm has lost both its ability to and interest in making comprehensively good development decisions. Due to attrition, in only three to four decades the structure of the development firm becomes the structure of the development industry. Currently, high-quality professional developers are on the endangered species list and we are within sight of extinction.

When we analyze the structure of the multi-family development firm, it's useful to view it as a machine. More specifically, it is a *complex* machine designed to create other complex machines, which we call communities. It is a factory for building. Reaching for their highest potential and most viable uses, these organizations have the ability to produce thriving communities that contain useful spaces for living, encourage commerce, and consequently deliver substantial profits to their entrepreneurial factory owners. But because the long-term viability of the community is not highly valued under today's prevalent merchant model, the factories that manufacture most of our communities are incentivized to design their own organizations instead as factories for raising capital and generating a high volume of low-grade building product.

The subtle but important shift between these two opposing organizational visions is that one is designed to use capital to create great communities and the other is designed to raise great sums of capital, resulting in the creation of buildings. One strives for greatness and achieves profitability and the other seeks profitability and achieves mediocrity.

Of course any firm can fail on an individual investment basis; that's the risk of entrepreneurship. Failure can come in the form of poor assumption, mistiming the business cycle, overly aggressive cross-collateralization or a myriad of other external forces. There is, however, a direct link between corporate structure and investment decisions. The likelihood of any catastrophic event occurring is an antecedent to the degradation of skills within and the structure of the firm itself.

By understanding the problems that plague our organizations, we are better positioned to contemplate the risks associated with our investments. From an organizational perspective, the problems often fall into one of two buckets:

1. *The outdated structure.* This issue that plagues us is often the lingering effects of an older firm that was designed to operate and solve problems that, due to the ever-changing development landscape, no longer exist. An example would be a firm that was designed to produce single-family homes and which now is focused on developing high-density condominiums or apartments. These two products have vastly differing challenges, which require completely different skill-sets and therefore should have fundamentally different structures. Likewise, a development firm that has evolved from relying on "country club" money to institutional equity will also require different levels of structural sophistication.

   Of course, organizations are somewhat organic and business models have a certain amount of elasticity. However, there is a significant danger to the quality and longevity of our firms when we choose to address these adjustments with a series of patches or Band-Aids. Too often, the periodic review of the organization's structure to ensure its efficient design gets placed aside in order to concentrate on the challenges of daily business. The fact is that organizational structure counts.

When the harmony between organization and product degrades, the firm's executives are no longer sufficiently protected and the business model no longer works efficiently to compete in the market.

2. *The wrong focus.* In younger organizations, the tendency to design the firm primarily for the acquisition of capital is rampant. These firms are often headed by former lawyers and bankers, whose connection to the industry is derived from a love of doing deals rather than a love of real estate development. It is not surprising that these firms pump out a lot of product that achieves the least amount of quality for the largest amount of return percentages. Bottom-line profits and myopic IRR-driven thinking take precedence while community concerns rarely enter the conversation.

For either of these situations to ever be rectified, the executive team must first recognize that there *is* a problem and second, come together to address the varied shortcomings of their organization's structure. We must remember that our intent is to restore or possibly create balance within the company. The implication of the "Outdated Structure" issue is that current firms are in a state of dilapidation due to their still-existing older and now defunct models. Regardless of whether it is actually true or simply an illusion, the impression exists that things were once in alignment and that there was once an integrity that has now been lost. Fixing an outdated structure is a quest to return the company to that state of harmony (or rather, restoring harmony to a new business model). This can be more challenging than it sounds because restoring integrity to an organization does not mean 'doing things the way we used to do them.' Our new business model has new challenges and our operating structure must be designed to address our present and future needs.

The latter situation, "The Wrong Focus," is the most challenging to fix because a firm designed with the wrong focus will almost always have also been built upon the wrong values. Because it was ill-conceived from the start, there is nothing substantial to which to return. Of course we are not saying that just because the company is built upon a weak foundation that there are not a number of positive attributes. However, to realize the potential of those positive characteristics, a framework must exist in which they may be exploited. This is where the owners are entering new and unchartered territory; where they must don their pith helmets, grab their machetes and forge a new path.

In each of these cases, whether it is an act of restoring or creating, the bedrock on which we will build our company is values. In chapters to come the importance of operating with the right values will be addressed at length. But at this semi-macro level, it is useful to establish the two types of values; universal and individual, and to distinguish between them.

The first classification, 'universal' values, are absolutely essential to each firm's success. They are:

1. To select investments that anticipate a real and reasonable profit to their investors.

2. To develop assets that contribute to the long-term betterment of the community in which they reside.

3. To structure an organization that is self-perpetuating.

The second classification, 'individual' values, are those specific to the leadership team. Individual values may target certain types of neighborhoods or demographics for investment or religious affiliation. Individual values may possess a component unique to its owner's beliefs or interests and the corporate culture they intend to perpetuate.

In either case, the adjustments to a firm's DNA will be a surgical procedure; the results of which may be manifold. It may require additional skill-sets or removing existing ones. It may require simply tweaking the business model or it may require a ground-up approach (this is likely the most feasible solution because so many of our decisions are intertwined and when restructuring, a blank slate is just wieldier). It may involve dumping certain product types or revenue streams. It may require significant investment. The only things certain are that such a revolution will require a deep discussion among the firm's leadership, and that difficult and fundamental operating changes must occur.

The Definition of Developer

It is in some ways difficult to distinguish the developer from the building. The building is, after all, the result of the developer's vision, efforts and investment. That said, we must also begin our enquiry by acknowledging that the buildings we create are simply a by-product of a sound system of development. We repeat: *buildings are simply a by-product*. As complicated as the process may be, the creation of a building is not terribly difficult. For 90 percent of the project's lifecycle, there are defined processes set by our funding sources, municipalities, architects and engineers, and finally through generally accepted construction techniques. Ninety percent of our job is process and 10 percent is art. It is within that 10 percent, however, that an opportunity exists to differentiate ourselves, our organizations and our profession.

Sadly, within most development organizations these days, the focus is on being excellent at the easiest 90 percent. These failing organizations we described are not actually development firms; they are project management factories. Consequently, they do not produce developers; they produce project manager lemmings.

Before we consider how to fix our organizations, we first need to look at the top of our corporate pyramid – the executives, or "developers." After all, this is the source from which the vision and direction flow. We must first establish the definition of a developer, what qualifies him as such, and what his role is within the organization before we can begin to evaluate his adequacy or suitability.

As we attempt to define who the developer truly is, we immediately see the clearest indicator that our industry has lost its way: there is no consensus as to the definition of a developer. Ask some current real estate developers to define the word. Most will look at you blankly, as though they've never contemplated the question, and then manage to list the string of tasks they regularly perform. Unfortunately, this strategy is wholly inadequate.

Wikipedia defines "real estate developers" as "the coordinators of the [real estate development] activities, converting ideas on paper into real property." That meek and passive definition is so offensive that it should inspire true developers to burn down and rebuild the entire industry. We've just been described as a bunch of secretaries. These days, that's not far from the truth, especially when you consider the dumbed-down trends in recent decades. The talents of would-be developers are molded into low-grade project managers. Wikipedia does go on to describe the activities of developers as to "…create, imagine, fund, control and orchestrate the process of development from the beginning to end." These are not the activities of a coordinator. They are the actions of giants, visionaries and entrepreneurial trailblazers. The dichotomy of these two opposing definitions underscores the fact that we are standing at a fleeting fork in the road. Right now, we have an opportunity to choose the path that our industry will take. But if we do not decide soon, the decision will be made for us.

In an attempt to glean the correct definition of "developer," the initial question should be: is the developer an individual or is the developer the organization in which they operate? The question may seem elementary and absurd, but when a development organization is built under the wing of a larger real estate services (RES) umbrella, the parent organization typically attempts to create a development group, which usually contains no actual developers.

We might ask ourselves how this is possible. Why would it ever be in the best interests of a large firm to have a development team with no actual A to Z real estate developers? There are quite a few answers to this question:

1. The personality of a true developer is less able to dovetail cleanly into a traditional corporate culture. This is because the personality traits common to the majority of real estate developers is grander than is palatable within many larger RES companies. Large organizations that seek the stability of a very typical corporate culture, may view the instability of the developer's temperament as an unnecessary risk.

2. By disassembling the skills of the developer into a series of lesser subject matter experts (SMEs), the loss of any individual is less disruptive to the organization as a whole. Additionally, the simplistic skills of SMEs are more plentiful and less costly to the organization.

3. Larger development firms whose primary focus is not development often do not hold real estate development in its highest esteem. They tend to value the acquisition of capital as the primary goal and accordingly seek development principals who share their values. These large groups have likely never evaluated their product from a community-enhancing perspective, so they wouldn't value that ability in a firm leader. Accordingly, a "fundable" résumé is more important than a comprehensively solid book of work.

So, is the developer the individual or the organization? Simply put, the industry excels *with* true developers in ways that it does not without them. The passion and brilliance that is embodied in the individual developer inspires all within our profession. Great buildings are inextricable from the men who create them. And even though there are many firms that produce many buildings, it is the authors' belief that the "developer" is absolutely an individual, and not a tax identification number or organization.

Now, let's ask ourselves: Which individual? And what makes them a developer? Conducting a simple survey of either industry insiders or the common public would almost unanimously define the developer as the firm's owner. More often than not, that is probably coincidentally true, but that answer may be too simplistic or even wrong. The owner of the firm tends to be its founder and/or the largest shareholder. So couldn't Warren Buffet invest the capital to create a development firm and retain majority ownership? (In fact, the authors would happily invite Warren Buffet to become one of their investors.) Would that somehow make him a developer? Is it simply taking the financial risk of the organization and its product that begets the title "developer?"

Many who have matriculated into the profession from the financial services industry might be inclined to answer affirmatively, but they would be as wrong as many of the buildings they create. Investment in real estate alone does not make one a developer; it just makes them a real estate investor. It's at this point that the schizophrenia of our situation becomes apparent.

Playwright Tom Stoppard put his finger on the issue: "Throughout our [professional] lives, we operate so close to the truth, who we are becomes a permanent blur in the corner of our eye, and when something nudges it from our periphery it is like being ambushed by a grotesque." The truth is right there for all of us to see, but a constant focus on the mundane tasks required in our profession has allowed us to forget what it is that makes us *us*.

In the same way that there is little agreement as to who the developer is, what makes one a developer is an equally elusive concept. About the only area in which consensus is achievable is regarding what tasks the developer regularly performs. The problem with rattling off a laundry list is that it fails to capture the essence of what it means to be a developer, because being a developer is greater than the sum of performing the activities of development. It's tragic that we know what we do, but not who we are.

Although we can definitively say that a developer takes his comprehensive knowledge of macroeconomics and finance, law and insurance, urban design and engineering, architectural and interior design, construction, leasing and sales and uses it to create, imagine, fund, control and orchestrate the process of development from the beginning to end, all we've done is describe a day-in-the-life of a developer in the form of a giant run-on sentence. The fact is that the developer must do all of this, but none of it defines him.

To reach the molecular understanding of what makes someone a developer, we need to take a much more Platonic approach. That requires distinguishing "developer" from "Developer." The

Developer is an ideal. Developer is an illusory concept in which our individual experiences and the things by which we are inspired are balanced with commerce and the public good. They are articulated and sculpted in the built world with wood and steel and stone and glass, of solid and void. Being a Developer is a goal; it is our life's journey. Therefore, the debate is over:

We become developers when we choose to marry what is inspirational in life with what is best for the public through a nimble use of our developers' toolset. We become a developer for a lifetime, and if we are lucky in the decades that follow, for a few of those moments we transcend 'developer' and become a 'Developer.'

Clearly, this definition derives from a place of great passion. But isn't it passion that we live for, that we should strive for each and every day? Isn't the loss of that passion in our lives tragic? Isn't it awful that when not guarded and protected, passion is replaced initially with apathy and eventually with resentment? When we lose the passion for our profession we are only working for money – and isn't that sad?

Now that we know who the developer is and what makes them a developer, we also know a number of tangential things. We know that the developer may own the company, or he may not. We know that within a good firm, everyone on the development team is either a developer or is a developer-in-training. We know that there are development firms that don't have a single developer in them, and that we can recognize them by the quality of their product. But more important than anything else, we know that we are developers, or can at least become them again.

Definition of Success

The developer was a once considered a great artist and entrepreneur, implementing his vision and taking risks with his capital. Presently, the developer has subjugated himself to being the lackey of investment bankers. The problem is that many developers have bought into the popular notion that success is simply measured by dollars earned. Of course this belief dictates how they build their organizations and how they train their employees, as we've discussed. Unquestionably, profit is a major reflection of any project's success. However, short-term profit for a few at the expense of the long-term experience of many is unacceptable. When we choose the opportunity to alter the face of our cities, we accept the responsibility to improve them. Therefore, it has become necessary to revisit what it means to be a successful developer.

Much effort has been expended by the authors thus far to describe the slow and imperceptible regression of skills and values that has led to the current state of the profession. Until now, we have been most concerned with the skills aspect of the equation, but the definition of success falls more squarely into the realm of values. And it is with the subject of values that the most difficult part of our journey back to greatness begins.

It is easy to say conversationally that the values within our profession have eroded without getting much pushback. Generally, those within the industry will nod in agreement without making a direct connection to the definition of success. Contention enters when we actually do make that connection, because most of us have never really done so, beyond focusing on making tons of money.

So rather than starting an argument by addressing the subject directly, a more circuitous approach might be more effective. Let's be pragmatists and simply look at what is built. After all, there is no better reflection of our values than how we spend our money and where we risk our fortunes. So let's make some reasonable observations on our drive home tomorrow:

1. When traveling through suburbia, it is clear that pedestrian traffic plays no part in the modern definition of success.

2. When slowly traversing any one of our nation's thousands of clotted corridors lined with single-tenant retail uses, it is clear that the adaptability of spaces does not register on the success-o-meter. Turning a McDonalds into a Hardee's does not count as an adaptive use.

3. When touring the majority of apartment communities built over the past 30 years, it is clear that the word community is a misnomer – or perhaps an inside joke – as the amenities are clearly not designed or positioned to ever actually foster resident interaction.

The list can go on ad infinitum. We cannot continue to espouse a series of values that are not reflected in our products without our honesty coming into question. It is at this the point in our conversation where excuses typically come into play and our external locus of control is evident. We blame the city planners for their lack of foresight and non-theoretical understanding of what it takes to develop land. We blame the zoning boards and county commissioners for succumbing to the ridiculous whims of the neighborhoods in which we want to build. We whisper blame our equity partners and their antiquated list of programmatic requirements.

And so on, and so on. Our failings are always someone else's fault.

In order to take back our profession, we must assume responsibility for the results of our poor decisions and commit ourselves to wiser choices in the future. If we view the degradation of the urbanistic quality of life of our neighbors as something outside of ourselves, then we can never hope to make a meaningful and positive impact on our cities. As real estate developers, we are the greatest influence on the beauty, efficiency and quality of life on our cities. Our first step therefore, is to recognize that we are 100% responsible for the sites we choose and the buildings that we create. Regardless of any external factor, good decisions can be made at every price point.

It's by taking responsibility for our past and our future that we shift the locus of control from an external to internal. With that act, we again take charge of our destinies. It is this empowerment that is the foundation upon which we can rebuild ourselves, our organizations and our profession.

But reclaiming an active role in our futures only allows us to be heroic; it does not redefine success. Understanding that real estate development has unique implications and effects on society requires that we take a broader view of our responsibilities, as they extend much further than simply returning a proscribed profit to our investors. We have a direct, verifiable and immediate effect on our communities. People drive by our decisions, they shop and drink coffee and build their lives in and around the boxes that we create, their children play in the yards and in the streets. Our successes and failures materially matter.

So when asked, 'What is success?' our answer must be lofty and heroic. Success is achieved when we "enhance the lives and experiences of the community, while returning a reasonable profit to our investors." And what is more heroic than making people's experience of the world better?

Chapter 4

Goals, Values and Vision

*"Men cannot be men – much less good or heroic men –
unless their actions have meaningful consequences to people
they truly care about. Strength requires an opposing force,
courage requires risk, mastery requires hard work, honor
requires accountability to other men. Without these things,
we are little more than boys playing at being men."*
– Jack Donovan

Revising the definition of success as we did in chapter 3 (to enhance the lives and experiences of community members while turning a reasonable profit to investors) and establishing who the developer *is* and *why* are critical early steps to take in our quest to restore the integrity of our profession. But we are still establishing the premises of our transformation; we are not yet ready to act. Our next quest is to reexamine, not only how our organizations are structured and behave, but most importantly, to explore how effectively this behavior is aligned with our (the leaders of the organization) goals, vision and values.

As we will soon see, self-examination is a thorny endeavor. It requires a level of personal honesty that is neither natural nor easy. So, as we wade further into that Rubicon, we approach the inevitable choice between fundamental change and discontentment. This is because the mind is not designed to un-learn, and once we are conscious of our firm's actuality versus its potential, proceeding down the current path unchanged is untenable. Soon, we will be faced with the overarching question: "Do we continue to ignore this growing call to arms and let our firm and our industry drift into the oblivion of Wall Street subservience, or do we commit to restore it to its previous grandeur?" For the future of our children, our cities and our society, we must believe we will choose the latter.

We must refortify our organizations by incorporating the skills and goals that inspire our dreams and perpetuate our profession for generations to come. To begin this process, let's revisit a few key concepts:

1. For a development firm to be successful, it first must be profitable. Conversely, our revised value statement acknowledges that success derives not only from financial returns. To achieve real and comprehensive success, we must respect the awesome responsibilities we have to communities in which we operate. We must understand the actual needs of those communities and strive to create product that is appropriate and responsive to the development's location, scale, density and product type.

2. For 90% of a project's life-cycle, there are defined processes set by our debt and equity sources, the municipalities in which we operate, our teams of architects and engineers, and finally, through generally accepted construction techniques. Therefore, 90% of a developer's tasks are governed by process and only 10% are art. It is within that 10% that an opportunity to achieve greatness not only exists but is entirely within our reach.

3. With each successive generation, development firms produce greater numbers of lower-skilled developers who consequentially deliver less responsive buildings and gathering spaces, because our firms are structured to train our younger generations to become middling project managers rather than A-Z Developers.

Culture

As we found when we discussed the definition of developer in chapter 3, there were conflicting schools of thought. The same is certainly true of the term corporate culture. Entrepreneur.com, in their Small Business Encyclopedia, defines corporate culture as "*A blend of the values, beliefs, taboos, symbols, rituals and myths all companies develop over time.*" Very simple and straightforward, this definition combines what we believe and how we act with a sense of history. Dictionary.com takes a more pragmatic approach and explains corporate culture as "*the philosophy, values, behavior, dress codes, etc., that together constitute the unique style and policies of a company.*" While true, this seems like the denotative view that a human resources manager might concoct.

Equally, if we were to ask a jargon-centric PhD candidate for Organizational Behavior, he would probably say something along the lines of "*Corporate culture is actually the organizational paradigm resulting from the culmination and interpolation of a company's processes, stories and symbols, power structures, organizational structures, control systems, rituals and routines.*"

That narcolepsy-inducing string of words is, of course, an example of why you never want to hire someone with a Ph.D.

For our purposes, corporate culture is the nexus of structure and values. When these two seminal components act in concert and with integrity, great things are possible.

The act of self-examination described above will almost invariably result in the unearthing of fissures in our organizational foundation. Whether these catastrophically affect the integrity of our firm will be determined on an individual basis. Realistically however, if our enquiry did not unearth the need for significant and consequential rebuilding, then we are probably not yet ready to continue reading.

Most often, the reestablishment of the firm as a values-based entity will precipitate an organizational realignment and possibly full-on overhaul. This can occur even at the cursory level of incorporating the universal values described in chapter 3. However, when the leadership team folds their mutually agreed upon personal values into the mix, the chasm between structure and values is typically astounding, since the organization was not designed to adopt a value set that was absent at its inception.

What we find when we seek to reestablish organizational harmony is that examination necessitates action. Returning to a previous analogy of the development organization as a complex machine that makes other complex machines; we are in no better position by creating a machine which efficiently produces bad developers than if we establish a poorly conceived organization populated with excellent developers. Both situations culminate in failure.

What then, is a reasonable goal? Most people would agree that company culture flows from its leadership. In an effective culture, every employee can articulate 'what we're about.' In an outstanding culture, even those who merely come in contact with the firm can tell us about its culture. Consider companies like Wal-Mart or Home Depot, or Hewlett-Packard (before the Compaq merger), or Chik-fil-a, which are some of the most famous examples of companies in which an outstanding culture drives the business model.

Now that we've set the goal to create a culture that's balanced with the intent of the firm, there are three fundamental tenets to which we must adhere:

1. The organization must have a clear definition of what it values and why.
2. These values must be inspirational and support the organization's mission and vision.
3. The executive team must consistently embody, reaffirm and celebrate these beliefs.

Mission

This chapter is designed to address one half of the corporate culture equation: values. We'll get to the second half, 'structure,' in chapter 6. In reality, the term values is much more complex than the ideals in which we believe. "Values" is a big-bucket concept comprised of three distinct components: goals, values and vision. By now, our methodology is becoming clear. In the past three chapters, we have addressed *seminal aspects* of societal and corporate culture without discussing them in *corporate cultural* terms. As we progress, we are fine-tuning our understanding of these components, so we are able to successfully implement them in our lives and our firms.

Goals

In principle, the definition of goals is no different for a company as it is for an individual or for a community or society as a whole. Our goals are the results or achievements toward which our effort is directed. Therefore in our conversation about corporate values, our goals are simply the results of successfully operating in accordance with our values.

Let's remind ourselves: chapter 3 discussed three values that we described as the universal values of a healthy company. These were:

1. Selecting investments that serve their investors.
2. Developing assets that contribute to the long-term betterment of the community in which they reside.
3. Structuring an organization that self-perpetuates through sound business practices and strategies.

With these values in mind, the universal goals of a company would be:

1. To make a profit.
2. To make our communities better.
3. To create a stable organization.

If this seems somewhat simplistic or repetitive, it is because we are illustrating the point that there is a close and direct link between the values that we espouse and the ends that we anticipate. Throughout the book, we have referenced 'integrity' in a context that is not its most typical. In most conversations, 'integrity' is interchangeable with 'honesty,' the word's connotative meaning. Honesty, however, is an example of integrity, not its definition. According to Dictionary.com, the denotative meaning of integrity is *the state of being whole, entire or undiminished*. For our purposes, the variant to add is: '*with all parts acting in concert*.' With this definition in mind, there should be very little daylight between our values and our goals.

As with the subject of values, outside of certain universal goals above, the individual goals of the organization should be personal and specific to each organization. These will be the result of discussions between the leaders of the organization about what the agreed upon individual values will be. The important concept to retain is that when debating and agreeing to a set of values by which the organization will operate, a parallel conversation must occur in which the goals of the organization must be delineated. Those goals must be tested against the question; 'will these values logically and likely lead to these ends?'

Values

Every society has been established with a series of basic values. In the United States, the second paragraph of Thomas Jefferson's document the "Declaration of Independence" begins: "We hold these truths to be self-evident, that all men are created equal, that they are endowed by their Creator with certain unalienable rights, that among these are life, liberty and the pursuit of happiness."

Has anyone ever written such a captivating, hard-hitting statement about values? Not only did Jefferson boldly take a stand, but his carefully crafted words established a common set of American values which coalesced citizens to a singular purpose and formed the basis of our war for autonomy. After thousands of lives were given in defense of these values and the war with England was won, another debate ensued and a new document, "The Constitution of the United States," was authored by James Madison. This manifesto was intended to turn a broader set of principles into a working and sustainable model for governance – a business model of sorts. Even now, more than 200 years later, Americans take the day off from work on the Fourth of July to reflect upon and celebrate these original values. This is because 'values' inspires and binds people together, and when applied appropriately, they establish loyalty.

In order to succeed under our expanded definition of success: *"To enhance the lives and experiences of the community, while turning a reasonable profit to investors,"* our new development organizations must be 'values' driven. And as we stated in the introduction of this chapter, what it values must be inspirational.

A great and disheartening exercise is to survey the websites and collateral of our current companies and our local competitors for their values statement. Probably the most common answer to the question, 'What do our organizations value?' will be, 'The creation of shareholder value.' But who is that phrase meant to inspire? Shareholders. While a necessary aspect of our daily efforts, the creation of shareholder value is perhaps the least inspirational value that anyone can espouse. We have to imagine that it was invented by some marketing consultant, and used as a placeholder until a real 'value statement' could but established, and then somehow it was forgotten and never replaced. It's a turd – never use it. Wars have been fought over values. The new world was discovered over values. Say aloud, "Come my brothers, let's go forth and give our lives for the creation of shareholder value!" Try to pick up a girl at the bar with your sexy job-creating shareholder value. It's just not going to happen – unless she is a shareholder.

In order to be effective, the values we espouse must connect with the intended audience at a very basic level. And while when it comes to expressing those values generally transparency is a good thing, it is certainly true that not every value will connect equally with every audience; we must choose which ones to highlight for the appropriateness of whatever conversation or presentation we find ourselves engaged.

The place where leaders typically fail when expressing their values is in understanding the nuance of focus. Many people travel through life viewing the world from their own perspective. Their focus is inward as is their system for evaluation. When we express ourselves from the inward perspective of 'this is how *I* feel' or 'these are *my* goals' then we run the risk of being ineffective. Most often, the goal of conveying ones values to an audience is to make a connection with them first, and inform them second. This is again, because the power of the topic of values has the unique opportunity to establish a lasting and actionable connection.

We should therefore approach the topic from an outward perspective, which we do by positioning ourselves as equal or similar to the audience: "*We* hold these truths to be self-evident..." not, "*I* hold these truths..." The implication that we *share* this belief with our audiences makes all the difference. We are already doing this in our daily work with clients and stakeholders. When we speak with their members, we don't tell them how our proposed building is going to make us millions, or that the first thing we plan to do with that money is buy a new Lamborghini – they wouldn't care and they'd likely be offended. Instead we tell them how we are going to solve their problems or improve their lives. Yet when we leave those meetings, we often forget to apply that outwardly-focused perspective to every aspect of our company. Sure, we still want that Lambo, but it only inspires us.

Fortunately for us, as real estate developers, we have been given a great advantage. What we do is intrinsically inspirational. It is just so damned sexy. We CAN inspire the masses with the product we create. In fact, it can be said that we are in the business of inspiration. An essential part of our success relies on our ability to inspire communities to allow to build, to inspire debt and equity sources to provide us the capital to build, and to inspire our internal teams to articulate our visions. When we sit down to establish our company's values, we just have to harness that energy, that rejuvenated definition, and ask ourselves, 'What is the greatest thing that I and my company believe in?' If our answer remains 'the creation of shareholder value'– then perhaps we should become accountants.

Beginning

Establishing a mission and value-set for your organization, while not overly complicated, can be actually quite hard. Throughout the process, you bombard yourself with questions like 'From where should I derive my Company's values?' and 'Which values are important?' Part of the initial challenge comes from our natural expectation that values originate somewhere outside of ourselves; that they are independent of us. They don't and they aren't. Your company values and your personal values are not discrete issues. In fact, if the leadership teams' personal values do not directly inform your corporate values, then an important opportunity is being ignored.

That said, the answer to the question 'Should all of my personal values be a part of my company?' is a resounding no. When we establish our corporate ethos, the values that we include still must pass the test from above:

1. The values must be clear.

2. The values must be inspirational.

3. The values must be implementable.

If our values fail even one of these tests, then they will fail to achieve their intended goals; which are to inform and to unify.

1. If confronted with some initial mental paralysis when approaching mission ideation, try the following steps: As with most things, we begin by beginning. So, let's begin by carving out time to engage in whatever activity calms your mind and encourages creativity. See what happens. (For me [Blaising], that meditative state comes from clipping myself into my road bike and riding. For my coauthor [Reese], that involves long runs). Our methods don't really matter as long as they accomplish their goal – to clear our minds of daily clutter and allow us space and time for creative reflection.

2. Clearly, freeform thought will only take us so far. It's time to sit down and write. Some people are more adept at generating ideas without stringent organization, while others thrive on regiment. The simple truth is that the most effective strategy is the one that we prefer. However, part of step two does involve bringing initial organization to the process. When this occurs, begin to segregate the list into two buckets, real estate values and personal values.

   From the real estate perspective, answer these questions:

   a. What are the type(s) of product in which we want to specialize?

   b. Are we 'mission-driven' demographically or ecologically?

   c. Will we have a defined geographic focus?

   d. Do we prefer long-term ownership or the merchant model?

   e. How large a scale and reach do we want to achieve?

f. What ancillary components do you envision to achieve your goals (i.e., construction, property or asset management, or brokerage)?

And from a personal perspective:

a. What role does religion or fitness or politics play in your life?

b. Do you 'work to live' or 'live to work?'

c. What would you need to achieve to feel 'successful' in life?

d. What level of importance do you give to travel or vacation in your life?

e. Are you charity or service focused? If so, with which causes?

f. List anything that inspires you.

The purpose of this step is to fill a sheet of paper or two. This is introspective idea generation. We're not worried about being *right* at this point; rather, we're just aiming for honesty. It's also important to make sure that each firm's leaders are undertaking the same exercise with the same seriousness. This is because, in the case that there are multiple leaders, the final mission and values message must be cohesive and fully embraced.

3. For every potential value on our list, we still must meet the three I's (identifiable, inspirational and implementable). Think of it as a form of values SWOT analysis. While each is important, pay particular attention to hurdle number two: the value must be inspirational.

Remember, the key to being inspirational is to understand the audience with whom you are attempting to connect. The value's focus has to be about 'them.' In the same way that 'maximizing shareholder value' is only inspirational to the shareholder (and therefore inappropriate for the firm's website), we must ask ourselves, 'Who am I trying to inspire with this value?' The acceptable categories will be one of the following: employees, prospective employees, the public or current or potential partners. Read the list from their perspective. Consider only their wants and goals and ask yourself if you have expressed the basic, simple truths about who your firm really is. Did you bind and draw your audience to a common purpose?

Some of the greatest, most inspirational values statements have occurred at times of great strife, because that is when they have been most needed. Wars are famous for the need for inspirational proclamations and perhaps the greatest inspirational orator of the last century was Winston Churchill. Recall his address to the English people: "We shall not flag or fail. We shall go on to the end. We shall fight in France, we shall fight on the seas and oceans, we shall fight with growing strength in the air, we shall defend our island, whatever the cost may be, we shall fight on the beaches, we shall fight on the landing grounds, we shall fight in the fields and in the streets, we shall fight in the hills; we shall never surrender." I

mean my God, don't you just want to go defeat some Nazis!?
OK, who is with us?

4. Invariably there will be values that you hold dear, but which
   do not adequately pass the test. For these items, drop them off
   the list. Purge with confidence.

5. Assemble the leadership team, compile the lists, look for the
   areas with the greatest correlation and sort the list according to
   the number of members in agreement with any particular
   value. It is usually easiest to take the low-hanging fruit off the
   table before debate ensues. As you progress down the list, give
   each subject honest consideration and discussion. Wash.
   Rinse. Repeat until you have a tight and well thought-out list.

6. What you are left with is list of mutually agreed upon values
   that you commit to adopting in all of your corporate pursuits.
   These are items you'll live by, market and teach. Compile the
   final list and have every member of the team sign it. Although
   what is being created may not be a formal contract, it is, at the
   very least, a pact amongst the owners.

   This level of formality may seem somewhat superfluous;
   but remember we're attempting to build sound, long-term
   organizations. None of us are static, and we are ever-changing
   and growing. As with a marriage, it's crucial to change and
   grow together. The last thing you want is to say is, "I never
   agreed to that," when it comes to your core corporate values.

Vision

Vision is a word we use quite often in this book. We refer to the developers' vision for a property, leading by vision, and selling that vision. Vision is also a word that is used so often (usually incorrectly) in life that it is at risk of losing its meaning. We hope to restore its impact, at least among this book's readership.

The challenge with vision is that it must be both a tangible thing (an action and a goal), as well as a certain perspective of the world (being inspirational). In the Churchill quote above, the vision would be 'to rid the western Europe of the Nazi threat'; and it was effective because it was an inspirational vision described in an inspirational way by a master orator.

However, to begin to understand the role of vision and its correlation with values, let's start with a simplistic definition of vision as the confluence of goals and values. In other words, "Here is where we are going because this is our task and this is what we believe." Everything we do professionally, large or small, should be a part of a corresponding vision. This occurs at both an organizational and a project level. Like a set of stacked Russian Matryoshka dolls, each fitting neatly within the next, every vision we create is connected to the next, and at a basic level must be cohesive with our companies' values.

When conveying vision, our strategy is similar to our approach to choosing our value set; it must be outwardly focused. Vision, like values, is meant to inspire (albeit on a more pragmatic level). We therefore must learn how to consistently speak to our audience's motivations in order to achieve our goals. For instance it's not difficult to surmise that a property manager wouldn't be driven by the same forces as a construction sub-contractor. That said, vision can, but does not have to, be something larger than life. Another way to describe vision is "direction combined with passion." Vision took us to space; it built the pyramids; it flew around the world for the first time.

Conversely, vision, unlike values, changes with each application. While our values statement can be chiseled in stone and mounted to our walls, our visions breathe only as long as the task or goal to which they are affixed. That said, our vision must reflect our values 100% of the time. We can uniquely apply vision to every aspect of our company:

- Vision is applied to our annual goals.
- Vision is applied to our individual projects and the teams that we form to implement them.
- Vision is applied to the individual career paths of our employees.

Leading through vision is not the same thing as being a visionary, at least not in a colloquial sense. Being a visionary has come to universally connote creativity. Vision, on the other hand, is the act of conveying both a task and a goal in a manner designed to inspire and extract the best efforts of those involved. Because most people don't have a comprehensive understanding of what is involved in leading through vision, there are probably more examples in which vision goes more wrong than right, due simply to user error. In fact, the failure of vision's effectiveness often boils down to a few very basic reasons:

1. The person imparting the vision doesn't understand their audience; or
2. They cannot distinguish between inspirational and cheesey (think Successories posters); or
3. The vision is not reasonably attainable.

I [Blaising] recall a situation I faced while working as Development Manager at a large Multi-Platform Real Estate Organization Offering a Diverse Range of One-Stop-Shop, Value-Added Services. That's *actually* what our C-Suite called it – and by the way, in case you haven't guessed, it meant absolutely nothing. (A word of caution to any young developers: if your leadership team ever provides this sort of description of the company – *run, don't walk*. Get your resume together. The titanic is being driven by MBA jargon, has hit the 'shareholder value' iceberg and is embarking on some sub-aquatic exploration).

This particular organization was comprised of five regional development groups, and we were holding our annual summit. The development teams were flown to Atlanta and were assembled in the meeting room of a local hotel for a day of presentations, team building, 'lessons learned' sessions, etc. A series of presentations were given by accounting departments, HR, the C-Suite, all with the goal of focusing our efforts and keeping us motivated.

All of this pomp was intended to culminate in the unveiling of a new development process tool. It was a real-time tool that would automate much of the development process and create automatic reports to the partners (not wholly unlike the 'Balanced Scorecard' initiatives of the 1990s). Our General Counsel quite proudly stood in front of us and declared, "All of development happens here, in this process tool," displaying his so-called accomplishment to us, in the way that a cat who just captured and killed a shrew would present it to his masters for approval.

I remember leaning over to our Regional Partner from Florida and whispering, "Are you fucking kidding me? Do they have no idea what we do?" He looked over, acknowledged my comment and shook his head as if to say, "Don't worry about it, just smile." I was slated to lead a discussion on large-scale soil remediation (sexy topic huh?) shortly after the 'new tool' unveiling. As a result of its misguided message, I truncated my presentation to a brief discussion of the intended subject matter and a much longer discussion on the topics of the romance of being developers and 'why we're all here.'

Following my topic on the itinerary, the Florida Partner took control of the room, and began with, "As you can see, I was intending to speak about -------, let's forget about that, I'm going to pick up on this last topic and…" From there he went on to drive the subject home, more eloquently than I had. The day was saved and we all left the meeting energized.

The anecdote illustrates the situation in which the vision was not inspirational to its intended audience. It had no choice but to fall very flat.

In any organization, those at each level are painting on slightly different canvases. One of our jobs as leaders of these organizations is to fully understand the world through our employees' perspective and occasionally get them to step back from their work and absorb the entirety of the collective composition. No matter how smart or capable, we need to be reminded that everyone on our teams is making a different, but equally valuable contribution, but that they don't necessarily care about what we care about. In fact, it is often important that they *don't*. And to get the most and best contributions from them, it is our job to care about what *they* care about – not vice versa. Harkening back to the anecdote above – no developer will ever be inspired by an Excel data modeling tool, no matter how impressive or even indispensable it is.

In the example above, there were additional challenges due to a misaligned structure (a topic which will be discussed in chapter 6). Within that company, the umbrella organization was owned by a property manager and led by a retired navy officer, an attorney and an accountant – none with a single hour's experience as a real estate developer. They didn't know what we did, nor did they care and as such, they didn't have the slightest inkling as to how to *inspire* us.

Considerable time will be spent on the subjects of leadership later, but we need to never that forget people choose their career paths for very different reasons. The only way to reach them is to speak to them from the places from which they are inspired. We can 'manage' from our perspective, but that will never deliver to us the best that they have to offer.

The Vision Package

One of the primary tools the authors developed, and firmly taught as a means for conveying vision at the project level is the Vision Package. (See Appendix A for the complete Vision Package.) The concept of a vision package isn't a new one, but we have designed what we feel is a more useful package than we had previously seen. Our Vision Package contains an introductory statement about the project, and then the location attributes, demographic and psychographic assumptions, lifestyle assumptions, and product assumptions. It is a comprehensive and categorical SWOT analysis.

The purpose of a traditional Vision Package is to 'sell' a project to the internal investment committee. For simplicity's sake, it's usually constructed as a bulleted list of assumptions that lead to a conclusion as to why this project is important to undertake. Our goal is to make its relevance work throughout the design of the project. And so our goal was to organize the Vision Package in such a way that it could be broken down into multiple packets that would inform each member of the O.A.C. team. The value is that it gives each member of the team a common endpoint or goal. We have to remember that the project team's goal is to articulate the developer's vision and assumptions.

One of the key components of the new Vision Package is an introductory narrative that would both entertain and create a very specific memory for the team. It is specific enough to define certain aspects of the vision, but, because it is ultimately rearticulated in each team member's mind and with the filter of their own experiences and prejudices, will still allow for the creativity that they require to satisfy their needs to contribute to the end-product. (We personally like this much more than distributing photographs that are more limiting to each team member's individual imagination.) Here's a brief vision statement for a mixed-use apartment complex that was to be built over a grocery-anchored retail platform.

> Imagine a beautiful modern masterpiece sitting proudly above the intersection of Piedmont Road and Garson Drive. Life and energy spill out onto the street from the retail and residential uses. Like you, attractive twenty and thirty somethings adorn the patio as if they are growing from the landscape like a group of lithe saplings – drinking frothy coffees or cocktails. Their black and gray outfits stand in stark contrast to the glowing white architecture. Evening approaches and the world around you is a backdrop of shades of blue and orange and purple and eggplant. Once inside, you ascend to an open second-floor lobby where people stand and talk, work on their computers, and play games. There is a slight, but discernible sound of voices coming from the restaurant bar below and somewhere behind you (although you can't tell from where) there is the low rhythmic thump of some upbeat music coming – possibly from the walls, possibly from some unseen sound system. The energy is palpable and everywhere. Are you living in a rental community or the W Hotel? Sometimes there is little distinction. But it's been a long day and you can't decide, so you head up to your apartment and relax, change clothes and grab a quick 45-minute run, or succumb to the rhythm and descend those stairs for a couple of drinks and a small plate. As your feet move forward and the floor level rises to meet your eyes, you know that there is only one way that this night will end...

Clearly the narrative relies heavily on the qualities discussed in this chapter. It both engages the reader and creates a mental image that will be interpreted differently by each individual from the team. In this case, we thought it best to use a sleek and stylish imagery that approaches and then retreats to an implied sort of soft porn, reflecting the mindset and lifestyle of those described in the demographical information that followed in the complete Vision Package.

It doesn't matter whether we consider our daily lives, our duties as parents, our corporate culture or our organization's mission; everything in life has the opportunity to be more meaningful, richer and more vibrant when we use as our base the building blocks of goals, values and vision. Not only do they inform our actions, but these three key components force us to view the world, not from the simple inward perspective of our own wants and needs, but rather from the perspective of those with whom we interact. This allows our impact to transcend the average or expected and become inspirational.

Chapter 5

The Litmus Test

"Every battle is won before it is ever fought." - Sun Tzu

For a book whose intent is to help developers refocus and reinvigorate themselves and their firms, it is probably somewhat striking that there has been no discussion of buildings. That's because development firms do not fail because of their buildings. Sure, they may make terrible buildings that fail, or terrible buildings that don't, or great buildings that fail, and so on. The reason we don't concentrate on the building is because it doesn't matter – not really. Most likely, the failure occurred long before dirt was ever turned. As we stressed in chapter 3, our buildings are byproducts of the system of developments that we create.

When we say that buildings typically fail before they even exist, it is because the correct answers were not asked before the choice to move forward was made. On one level this is not surprising, since we only created our new, comprehensive definition of success two chapters ago. And, if the new definition of success for our firms is "to enhance the lives and experiences of the community, while returning a reasonable profit to our investors," then what is the definition of failure? Failure is not the opposite of success. Failure is the absence of it. We fail when we ignore (or worse, purposefully subjugate the needs of the community or our investors to our selfish wants) our responsibilities to those we're trained to serve.

Much effort has been dedicated in the previous two chapters to widening our gaze when it comes to our understanding of success and failure, our responsibilities as developers and the purposeful creation of value-sets. Individually, none of these items will make a better building. Collectively, however, they give us a base from which to behave in the business of creating more successful buildings. If the nouns *values and vision* are not proficiently understood, we cannot hope to implement them as verbs.

Most firms create values to act as slogans for their websites and advertising. We've all seen them: "People are our number one resource." "Doing well by doing good." While some are better than others, each is merely just advertising. We all know that Tide "gets the stain out" or that "Snickers satisfies you" and BMW manufactures "the ultimate driving machine," because that's what we've been told. But no slogan means anything if it is not backed up by performance. We will only accept these tag lines if Tide actually *does* remove the stain or if our BMWs actually do handle well. As such, our new goals must be verifiably implementable.

For our values and goals to translate to our building product, they must be actively present in every aspect of the process, from its inception. But really, what does that mean to be able to identify a value-set in a building? Certainly not every value has a physical component? That's true, but our collective values do inform the physicality of what we create. For instance, let's say that we have chosen the clichéd value: "Our people are our greatest resource." If implemented well within the organization, then a predictable result would be happier employees and fewer turnovers. Reduced turnover equals less chaos within the organization. And at a project level, consistency of leadership and implementation equals consistency of vision, which will result in more cohesive buildings. In other words, any value, when fully embraced and integrated, will have an effect.

In early 2007, my co-author and I were asked to take over a project that had been purchased and designed as a 312-unit building with a mix of condominiums and apartments segregated by a parking deck. Because the for-sale market was in clear decline, the condo portion needed to be dropped and the project had to be reprogrammed as an apartment complex. While the site was excellent, the design was atrocious and neither of us wanted to have our names associated with it. After some consideration, we proposed to our regional partner that we take over the project under the condition that we would get an extra four months and a redesign budget. This would have resulted in roughly $800,000 in additional costs. To our surprise, he agreed. The project was re-visioned and redesigned.

Then in March 2008, while site work was underway, I left to start my own firm and my co-author followed three months later. The project was handed off to a development manager within the firm. While he unquestionably did the best he could when it came to making value engineering decisions, choosing final color combinations, etc., he was too far distant from the seminal vision of the project to adhere to its spirit. The project was completed and leased up fairly successfully, considering the economic climate at the time. It is a good building, but it is no longer great. The chaos of project leadership turnover resulted in a loss of integrity for the community.

Beginning by Beginning

Although much of what is discussed in these chapters seems logical enough, we would expect it all to be very easily achievable. We might even be wondering why it isn't currently happening. As we described in chapter 1, the state of our profession did not happen overnight. The apathetic regression to designing our firms to serve as factories for low-grade building product has been a gradual, four-decade decline. And while we may not have been active participants in this degradation, we have at the very least been passive accomplices. Most likely, the generations that are poised to lead our firms into the future have never experienced the power of the heroic developer in action. They cannot easily implement these obvious concepts, because there are few mentors or models to follow.

Currently, we sit, stagnate and choose to not address the issues that plague us, even as we watch a very important window closing. Once the A-Z developers' retire and we are left with a conglomeration of SMEs, the model that we must replicate to save the industry will be lost forever. Our reaction of stagnation is neither surprising, nor is it a condition unique to real estate development; it is human nature. Beckett inadvertently captured this paralysis in what may be one of the best plays of the 20th century, "Waiting for Godot," whose final act ends as follows:

ESTRAGON: 'If we parted? That might be better for us.'

VLADIMIR: 'We'll hang ourselves tomorrow.' (*Pause.*) 'Unless Godot comes.'

ESTRAGON: 'And if he comes?'

VLADIMIR: 'We'll be saved.'

[Stage Direction] Vladimir takes off his hat (Lucky's), peers inside it, feels about inside it, shakes it, knocks on the crown, puts it on again.

ESTRAGON: 'Well? Shall we go?'

VLADIMIR: 'Pull on your trousers.'

ESTRAGON: 'What?'

VLADIMIR: 'Pull on your trousers.'

ESTRAGON: 'You want me to pull off my trousers?'

VLADIMIR: 'Pull ON your trousers.'

ESTRAGON: (*realizing his trousers are down*). 'True.'

[Stage Direction] He pulls up his trousers.

VLADIMIR: 'Well? Shall we go?'

ESTRAGON: 'Yes, let's go.'

[Stage Direction] They do not move.

CURTAIN.

The revelation that developers have important responsibilities to the communities in which we build only matters if that knowledge becomes manifest in action. As Vladimir and Estragon found above, making the choice to begin is much easier that the actuality of beginning. Fortunately, we can rewrite our situation.

Godot has arrived. With a plan.

So far, the primary problem we've discussed has been the effect of the shift of power from the developer to the investment banker: how that has changed our goals, our understanding of success and our responsibilities, and finally, the ways in which we build our firms. We have focused on this singularly because it is the root problem, and truthfully many of our troubles stem from it. It is not, however, the *only* major problem. If we expect to achieve any level of success in restoring our profession, there is a second issue that must be addressed: Our reliance on others to choose the sites on which we build.

During the building boom of the past few decades, fewer and fewer developers have actively targeted, assembled and entitled the properties on which they build. Increasingly often, we have relied on brokers to identify sites and market to them, allowing us to focus on more easily developable sites with less upfront risk and presumably shorter overall time-to-market lifecycles. In turn, we focused our efforts on the capital raise and implementation. We have subtly shifted our efforts from raising capital to develop important projects for our communities to finding developable dirt to fill our expanded capital pipes. This has changed everything.

While the organization obviously benefits by removing project risk wherever possible, our consistent reliance on the broker for deal-flow also tarnishes the firm's overall competence. We have neglected the key skill of land assemblage that is necessary to every good developer to the point that it is not contained in many firms.

This is one of the primary proficiencies necessary to call one's self a developer. As above, if this skill is not housed within the organization, it cannot be taught to future generations of developers. The results of this loss include:

1. *We abdicate control of our site selection to brokers.* Of course real estate brokers perform a valuable service within our industry, but site selection isn't one of them. The choice of determining the exact right site for a proposed project is the job of the developer. We are the creators and risk-takers. They are the conduit. Only the developer is implicitly tasked to be concerned with the betterment of the community. So while brokers are our friends and we enjoy playing golf or taking in a baseball game with them, we have to remember that the developer is the artist and the broker is one of our many paintbrushes. And the paintbrushes don't tell the artist where to paint.

2. *We accept secondary or tertiary locations because they require less work.* Laziness on the part of the developer becomes a malicious act when we fail to identify the best sites for our intended use. Our responsibility is always to do our best for the communities we serve. Throughout this book we describe locations or building products as 'better,' 'more appropriate,' and 'superior' or 'responsive.'

   But we're not talking about aesthetics or achieving proforma rental rates. For a development to be 'better,' it requires the confluence of the correct scale, the optimal location within the community and market timing. After all, if we correctly determine that a neighborhood needs an additional 300 apartment units, it will also need them in a specific location and at an appropriate time. By simply accepting the sites that are most easily assembled or entitled, rather than methodically selecting and acquiring the ideal location, we reject the value of a logical and cohesive urban fabric. After all, the 'right' site may not correspond to the location of an under-utilized shopping mall with the necessary existing land use designation.

3. *We fail to train our future developers.* The young developers in training that work for us will one day own their own firms and be tasked with doing their own developments. If they are never taught how to choose, assemble and entitle properties, then we can be assured that they will one day make our town and cities uglier and more disjointed.

The only way for us to achieve success is to take the lead in site selection. Use brokers as needed, but direct *them* to what *we* want assembled.

The Litmus Test

Improving the industry is not as simple as making one or two or three shifts in the way that we approach our profession. Our loftier goals will not be easily achieved. And while numerous changes must occur as we attempt to "right the ship," they will generally fall into a few larger buckets that we think of as our greater principles. Site selection, for example, is a subset of the question 'Which projects should we be implementing?' The answer to this question will be different for each firm, based on size, location, funding vehicles, focus and values. But within all this differentiation lies a common methodology. We'll call it our litmus test.

Most of us will say that our firm already *has* a litmus test. But upon examination, we'll likely find that is does not extend much further than 'Is the project fundable?' Moving forward, in order for a project to be viable for our firms, it should meet a greatly expanded series of conditions. Put in the form of questions these are:

1. Is the project financially viable?

2. Does the proposed project tell an important story for this exact site and the community in which it will reside?

3. Does the scale of the proposed project enhance the city at an urban level?

4. Is this the right location for the proposed project?

Regardless of the individual development tolerances that our firms choose, if the projects we pursue always meet the criteria we set for ourselves in this test, we will always be better positioned to achieve success.

LITMUS TEST QUESTION #1: Is the project financially viable?

Real estate development is an inherently capital-intensive endeavor. Our three primary components – land, materials and labor – are each intrinsically expensive. And of course there is also the fourth cost component – time, often the most critical difference between success and failure in any development project. So when the developer sits down to analyze the viability of his potential venture, he views his data through two lenses: financial analysis and market analysis. Each exploration answers a very different question:

1. The financial analysis tells us whether we CAN fund the project.
2. The market analysis tells us whether we SHOULD fund the project.

Most development firms are adept at addressing the first question. It's the most straightforward and definitive of the two. After all, if the project is not fundable, the project will never happen. That seems simple enough.

Financial Analysis

The tool the developer uses to perform this analysis is the proforma. Development firms utilize varying technologies and formats for their proforma analyses, depending on their product sector, the sophistication of their firm and funding sources, and the size of the projects that they undertake. Some use Argus, others use Excel, and others even rely on cocktail napkins.

Even though the proforma remains the greatest and most accurate tool for financial analyses, it does come with some significant risks. The first major problem is its inherent inaccuracy. The proforma is not an absolute, nor is it a continuum; rather it is simply a point, a dart on the board, a fictitious moment in time. It's a series of best guesses based on experience and available inputs that gets adjusted a hundred times, until an agreement is made between the developer and his debt and equity sources. Then it becomes a budget. The second major problem is the mistaken notion that the proforma is development. If that were the case, then the firms with the best proforma would also be the best developers.

The major mistake that many developers make lies not in their reliance on their proforma to make sound development decisions, but rather in their understanding of the role that the proforma plays in creating successful developments. The proforma is just the complex, agreed-upon language that allows the builder and the banker to communicate. Even once the final proforma is established, it is not necessarily any closer to 'correct' than any other. The real accuracy of a proforma lies in the experience and integrity of the one who creates it. Therefore, the analysis tool is inconsequential compared to the operator.

If the goal of financial analysis is to assist the developer, investor and banker in establishing the best bets within their respective risk tolerances, then two changes must occur. First, the developer must regain their A to Z skill-sets so that their numeric inputs are tempered with experience and wisdom. Second, the financial partners must require a greater investment risk from the developer. The problem is that reduced risk has incentivized the developer to tell the banker what he needs to hear in order to get funding. It's easy to disassociate ourselves from the fact that even mutually agreed upon lies are malicious when investors lose money. It is still theft. Until we are equally yoked in the success or failure of a project, the temptation on the developer to forego integrity is great.

Market Analysis

Market analysis consists of two primary focuses: micro-market and macro-market. The micro-market analysis relies upon correctly establishing the needs and stability of the street, neighborhood, town or city in which the project will reside. Questions 2 through 5 of the Litmus Test are designed to inform the micro-market analysis. As such, these issues will be more fleshed out in later pages.

The macro-market analysis, on the other hand, focuses on the larger questions of national and world economic trends. Because the focus of macro-market analysis is financial, the primary area of concern is the capital markets. This is where we attempt to triangulate our position within business and building cycles, identify the risk of bubble economies and forecast future cost of capital trends. Macro-market analysis is the acknowledgement that we operate within a much larger marketplace in which many forces exist well beyond our locus of control.

Two of the main reasons that a macro-economic understanding is critical to our strategic efforts are that: (1) our projects are inherently less liquid than many competing types of investments, and (2) our investments have typically greater lifecycles. It may take two to ten years for a projected investment to go from land acquisition through disposition. In that time, a bubble can emerge and burst, we can have three different presidents and administrations, or the European Union could disband. Time adds risks and potential chaos.

An easy position to take as the developer is that we have financial partners to rely on for the understanding of world and capital markets. While they are certainly a valuable input, there is a single major difference between us and our debt and equity partners: risk. Remember. While we may be partners, we are not the same. They aren't investing their own money. Even though they certainly want us to succeed, if we don't, they are only partially risking their bonus. If things go poorly with our investments, they might lose their jobs, but we can lose our houses.

With the goal of long and prosperous careers in mind, we must absolutely observe, understand and respect the market forces that are greater than our individual spheres of influence.

As we stress the importance of a firm grasp of macro-economic theory for the developer, we do recognize that our entire audience is not comprised of closet macro-economists. For someone who has never studied Keynes or Minsky, the subject matter can be quite dry. There are ways to make the process more enjoyable and results even more robust. For instance, popular culture tends to mirror the social condition and a sort of zeitgeist approach can make the process more palatable. By pairing these dryer texts with something more lively like biographies of important figures of the time (in the case of Keynes, Winston Churchill or Franklin Roosevelt or JP Morgan, etc.), or popular social fiction from authors like Fitzgerald, Steinbeck or Eliot, one can really get a sense of the societal perspective. Period movies are also great sources to understand the social outlook of the time (although we are strictly referring to movies made during the time that we are discussing and not recent movies made about those times). The importance is in gaining a comprehensive understanding of how our societies and economic systems really work. So if a 'spoonful of sugar makes the medicine go down,' then by all means add the necessary candy. Supplement the studies in whatever way works.

LITMUS TEST QUESTION #2: *Does the proposed project tell an important story for this exact site and the community in which it will reside?*

Every project that a developer chooses to undertake establishes a baptism for that site; it is an act of renewal. Insofar as it is also a piece of a neighborhood and city, that relationship extends to a much greater tapestry, albeit to a lesser degree. Whatever this land has been in the past is erased and a new life and opportunity begins. As such, each building or park or parking lot has both a purpose and a use with which the local inhabitants will engage, physically or visually. In this way, as developers, our work tells a story about a community's needs at a specific moment in time. And because the projects that we envision and construct have substantial cost, these stories also have longevity. Our most successful buildings are a testament to our vision for a site that will last for years to come – and so are our failures. Because our physical impact on the city is greater than with most professions, so is our responsibility to the communities in which we work.

Fortunately, we do not reinvent the language of development with each project. After all, towns, cities and urban cores have been built and rebuilt for almost 400 years in America and for centuries longer in Europe. So no matter the type of project we conceive for our site (even if we are founding a new town in the middle of a cornfield in Iowa), we have access to a plethora of successes and failures throughout the world. Functionally, urbanistically and aesthetically, we have an extensive dataset of what has worked and what has not. The developer's challenge is to understand how to interpret each aspect of the data and use it to tell his story.

The story that we tell we tell as developers is always one of appropriateness. Appropriateness in this context comes down to the answers to these questions:

1. Functional. Does the city or neighborhood need the service or function that we propose?

2. Urbanistic. Will the proposed project strengthen or enhance the public's experience of the neighborhood?

3. Aesthetic. Will the proposed project work visually within the context of the neighborhood?

This particular enquiry gets a bit squishy, because there is no one right answer. Our cities need many different services and there are multiple ways to develop a site that will enhance the neighborhood functionally and aesthetically. There are a few right answers on every site, and many more wrong ones. That said, our goal is to separate the wheat from the chaff and consistently arrive at one of the sparser right answers for each aspect of the appropriateness story we're constructing.

1. *Appropriateness of function.* There is a phrase 'When you are a hammer, everything is a nail,' which aptly describes one of the challenges that we developers face on a regular basis. After

all, nothing excites us more than finding an open or decaying plot of land. When we see this condition, we see opportunity. We see dollar signs. Our task in this question is to see past our own needs and look to the greater good of the neighborhood.

Of course, our ego tells us to build where and whenever possible, but we must force ourselves to answer the more important questions: Does the city need our retail or residential project? And does it need it in this location? We must develop the restraint to *not* build, just because we can. So construct a story about how life will be different and enhanced because we choose this time and this location to make our unique mark.

2. *Appropriateness of urbanism.* Because almost every site has a connection with a public street or space, there is an opportunity to affect the urban fabric. Whether it is building a structure to the lot-line to reinforce the streetscape, pulling the building back for a patio or garden, adding a sculpture, or creating a pass-through to connect otherwise separated areas or the neighborhood, we, as developers, make choices which can enhance others' experiences.

The easy answer when programming a site is to maximize our F.A.R. in the name of economics and efficiency; but once again, this is a place to look past our own selfish perspectives and consider the short and long-term needs and experience of the community.

3. *Appropriateness of aesthetic.* Aesthetics is one of those subjects where most people (development industry or not) say

'There is no right or wrong, just opinion.' It's a phrase that is typically used as a cop-out by developers to compensate for their lack of aesthetic training and taste. Aesthetics is the science of composition and proportion (objective, not subjective) and there are absolutely degrees of right and wrong. The developer's job is not necessarily to be an expert at crafting masterful facades, but he must possess aesthetic vision for the project. He must be able to answer basic questions about the societal role of his building. Once a developer knows how the building should be positioned, he can then hire the appropriate team with the aesthetic acumen to execute his vision.

Hopefully, we will develop enough vision and sense to counteract one of the more insidious trends within the development community: hiring a mammoth firm as a one-stop shop, simply because it is easier to manage. While there is certainly the advantage of ease of communication and coordination within the design team for rapid changes and a tighter, safer set of documents, the assembly of these various skills under a single umbrella often occurs at the detriment of the design. The architect's business plan shifts from designing the best product for his client to creating the most efficient, and profitable commission for himself. There is a value to the inefficiency of the creative process. After all, it certainly makes sense that the best architect for the design of an infill brownstone building in a historic district would be different than for an ultra-modern commercial building in a trendy warehouse district.

So before we choose our team, we should ponder the future building's character. Our first question is: 'Is this building going to be an object building or a fabric building?' These are architectural terms which essentially differentiate buildings whose functions signify events within the city and should therefore draw attention to themselves through their scale and aesthetic (objects) and those whose function helps to tie the city together (fabric). Traditionally, churches, governmental buildings and monuments would be object buildings and most else would be fabric.

Over the past few decades, developers have concentrated more on object buildings than fabric, and a legion of urban planners attribute this shift to the growing disjointedness and lack of continuity within our cities. We have chosen to ignore the fact that our work has a reciprocal contextuality. As developers, we are always stitching a small section in a much greater quilt and must possess the dexterity to understand our work within that greater framework. After all, when everything is special, nothing is special.

The secondary aesthetic questions that must be answered by the developer regard the look of the building: will it address the past, the current context, or the future of the community? On a macro-level, the developer should have an understanding of where the neighborhood has been, as well as a vision of where it is going. This vision is not necessarily what *we* want it to be as much as what it (and its inhabitants) wants to be. Development that is not user-centric is a failure. The 20th century architect Louis I. Kahn once said (alluding to Plato's theory of forms):

And if you think of Brick, for instance, and you say to Brick, "What do you want Brick?"

And Brick says to you, "I like an Arch."

And if you say to Brick, "Look, arches are expensive, and I can use a concrete lentil over you. What do you think of that Brick?"

Brick says, "... I like an Arch."

Our primary job as the great artists of our cities is to understand what a site and neighborhood wants to be; and our secondary job is to marry that with our own vision for its future function and aesthetic. And of course our solutions fold in tremendous amounts of practical data, which include demographic trends, economic forecasts, other work underway in the neighborhood, and the comprehensive plan established by local planning departments.

LITMUS TEST QUESTION #3: Does the scale of the proposed project enhance the city at an urban level?

In our opening chapter, as we discussed the growth and migration trends of the American city, we acknowledged that cities generally grow. Of course, there are expansions and contractions with economic cycles and population migrations. And cities that have diverse industrial revenue streams tend to absorb these fluctuations better than those who do not. (Detroit is a prime example of a city so tethered to the auto industry that changes in competition and innovation in transport effectively destroyed the city for 30-plus years.) But a few anomalies aside, cities do tend to grow. As growth occurs, resources become more limited, and in a market economy, more expensive. It therefore logically follows that as we redevelop properties, we must also increase scale. In other words, things will get bigger.

While all of this is correct, there must be logic in place as to the amount that something increases in scale with each iteration of redevelopment. By *logic* we mean a force that understands and accepts economy, yet resides above it. In many cases, the answer to this is managed by our local municipalities through zoning codes and master plans. Of course, tension often exists between the forward-looking nature of the developer's vision and the stagnant, often outdated zoning codes, as well as with the typically reactionary neighborhoods. This incongruity of purpose is the source of most developer's ulcers and high blood pressure. The authors would posit that there is a likely correlation between the variance process and the developer's blood pressure. So when we do choose to traverse that gulf between the local entitlements and the economic reality of getting a project done, the developer must address the question of appropriateness of scale. We must craft a story about the short- and long-term health of the community.

Because the developer will always face the constraints of zoning, entitlements and potentially regressive neighborhoods, we must possess a sense of realism that tempers our own selfish desires. This is easiest to do when our wishes are much greater than the tolerances of our site's entitlements. In this case, we are restrained by a zoning code. The real test of our mettle comes when scale is not constrained. This is where we must choose between what we desire and what is appropriate. This is where the great Developer chooses to build what he *should*, rather than what he can.

There are wonderful examples of cities that have gone through multiple iterations of redevelopment and retained the greatness of their character. The illustrations of Manhattan over the past five centuries shown in Figure 1 are a compelling illustration:

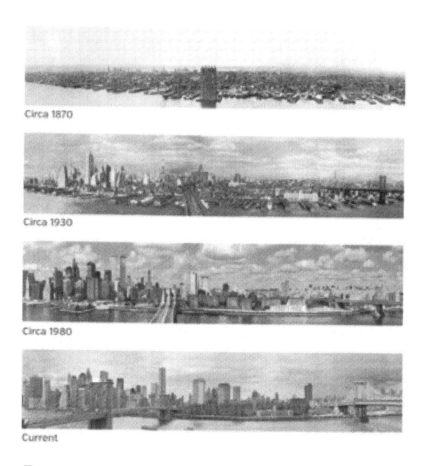

Figure 1. Manhattan: 150 Years of Growth

On the other hand, a vivid example of a developer's apparent disregard or even disdain for the good of the community is a condominium tower in Atlanta, Georgia called "The View at Chastain Lofts." Completed in 2005 near the height of the housing boom, this 10-story condominium complex reeks of mediocrity and deficiency in every regard. It is an aesthetic blight in an inappropriate location and is completely out of scale with its surrounding context. At the time the building was proposed, one could imagine the developer arguing that it was 'a pioneering building that opens the way for a future high-density residential pocket' – but one would be wrong. Lewis and Clark, this development is not. See Figure 2 for two photos that illustrate how inappropriate the building is for its surroundings.

Figure 2. Getting Development Wrong:
The View at Chastain Lofts, Atlanta, Georgia

The project is located at the apex of a hill on a busy corridor and is set within a sea of aging, medium-density retail. The views of Buckhead are excellent (provided that you don't look down at the sea of surface parking and air handlers). On paper, a developer could easily write an investment package and couple it with a gleaming proforma, which could sell the vision to overconfident bankers caught up in the throes of a real estate bubble they didn't understand.

But a simple drive past the site should have dispelled all questions about whether or not the proposed scale was appropriate. Ten seconds worth of thought about the psychology of the buyer would have convinced even a layman that the sales proposition was weak. And a moment's concern for the surrounding community's character and future needs would have led the developer to understand that the plan was disrespectful to its residents. None of these issues must have ever come to mind.

Fortunately, in the case of "The View at Chastain Lofts," the market agreed, sales efforts were a failure and the building eventually went to auction. One would hope this experience would be a black eye that would cause the developer to put more thought into his investments before inflicting them upon the market. However, the building exists, the blight remains, and residents will have to pass this abomination every time they travel through Buckhead on Roswell Road for decades to come. The damage is done.

There are also spectacular examples of appropriateness of scale. We must understand that the term *scale* does not simply mean that all developments should be the height or size of their surrounding neighbors. Some uses may call for the buildings to be much larger or smaller than their contexts. There are ways for a building ten times larger than the average buildings in the community to still feel appropriate to the neighborhood.

One of the greatest urban laboratories for a community with varying sizes, scales, styles, and typologies mixing together and retaining both richness and appropriateness is on Newbury Street in Boston's Back Bay (see Figure 3). There exists a mixture of retail, residential, commercial and civic uses that work harmoniously. Classic townhomes are juxtaposed with ultra-modern storefronts and they all seem to work themselves together into an amazing tapestry that both serves the public need and is comfortable to their sensibilities.

Figure 3. Vistas Along Boston's Newbury Street

Many books have been written about the neighborhoods of Boston, and the urbanism of the Back Bay is certainly a known, but not a wholly unique quantity. There are cities throughout America that act as a model for good mixed-use urbanism. It's our job to visit Boston, New York, Chicago, San Francisco, Washington DC, Philadelphia, Savannah and Charlotte (and many more here and abroad).

We must experience the conditions that we seek to replicate. Our success relies on having sat in these spaces and felt and observed them to know what 'appropriateness' truly means. It is easy to forget, when toiling over spreadsheets, selling ideas to investors, touring potential developments sites and the many tactical items that fill our calendars that we are creating experiences. To make the best decisions, we need to slow down to enjoy and understand the environment.

LITMUS TEST QUESTION #4:
Is this the right location for the proposed project?

Another great challenge that we face as developers is discerning between a 'right or wrong' location. More often than not, we are directionally correct, but the ability of every single developer to consistently identify the best location (even if it isn't available) is clearly lacking. As we discussed previously, one of the aspects of being great developers is acquiring all of the skills necessary to consistently perform great development.

Unfortunately, one of the key development skills that many developers have outsourced in recent decades is site selection. Rather than personally choosing our assemblages and performing or hiring others to put it together for us, we have instead come to rely on brokers to find and aggregate the easiest options. We sit and wait for marketing packages to be emailed to us, and then fight in an unnecessary feeding frenzy with other developers as we compete to pay the most for what may not even be our ideal site. It simply makes no sense.

The results of not showing proper respect for location vary from less profitable projects to potential harm to our neighborhoods. We need to view our land assets in the same way that we do the rest of our assets. Every deviation from the ideal investment introduces a level of risk. And while obtaining the ideal site is clearly not a realistic choice every time we undertake a development, we need to be able to identify what is 'ideal' every time and then manage and understand the real potential effects of deviation from it. Typically, location risks challenge either money or time, and in the case of some investments, both. Even placing aside our responsibility to the community for a moment, from a selfish perspective, the developer must be more aware and averse to investments that endanger our wealth.

With each question in the Litmus Test so far there has been a discussion of the macro versus micro perspective, and much of the focus has been on reminding us to incorporate that macro view into our decision-making process. The subject of location probably makes the most obvious case for the argument that every aspect of our influence is a small part of a much larger composition.

Which is why the analogy of the developer as a great artist painting on a giant canvas is most apt. For decades, we developers have increasingly concentrated our efforts like Monet, stippling away with our faces only inches from the medium. However, without the perspective gained from stepping back from the canvas and taking in the bigger picture, we never create our own 'Water Lilies.' Our cities instead often resemble more of a Rorschach Test. We all know that wonderful scene from the film 'Ferris Bueller's Day Off' in which the characters are at the Art Institute in Chicago, gazing at Seurat's 'A Sunday Afternoon on the Island of La Grande Jatte.' We would do well to remember it in our daily work.

The subject of site selection is also the area in which most developers will push back against the authors. Each of us believes that we 'know land' and that we already consider our developments from multiple perspectives. However, based on the number of sufficiently misplaced developments that line our streets, one must assume that we either rarely consider the context of our art, or that we are just really bad painters.

Conclusion

With every project that we consider undertaking come hundreds of questions that must be asked and answered. And not all questions are created equal. The purpose of the Litmus Test is to establish a set of gating questions, which act as the initial foil in our decision tree. If all four of the Litmus Test questions cannot be answered satisfactorily, then either the vision of the project in some aspect must change, or perhaps the project should not currently be pursued.

On the surface, the methodology is straightforward and logical. In fact, it may even seem elementary. But if we were to take a critically honest look at the composition of our firms, we would likely have to admit that:

1. We are not all individually expert at answering each of these questions, and

2. Our firms do not typically have an expert on each of these questions in-house.

In the case that we actually do possess real expertise in each of these areas, our processes and organizations still aren't structured in a manner to leverage these talents to their fullest for each project that is proposed at the particular time that the expertise is most needed. Our machines are not yet efficient. Outside of the elder members of our most sophisticated firms we have replaced the A to Z developer with subject matter experts (SMEs). These are single-subject (typically finance) project managers who we mistakenly call developers. We may even be SMEs ourselves. But being both an SME and a leader of the firm is not necessarily its death-knell, as long as we understand and respect the expertise of the others who address our own deficiencies.

So what is the solution? Do we add new partners to round out our expertise gaps? Do we dissolve our companies and reform new entities that are aligned to make better, safer long-term decisions that will bring more consistency to the firm? Both solutions will work, and both will be difficult. This is in part why we began the book with exercises to align the vision and values of the organization. Unless each member of the leadership team is wholly bought into the goals of the new firm, this step will be impossible to tackle. The firm will either die or these initiatives will be shelved. We cannot halfway fix our firms.

A conglomeration of loosely-tethered SMEs, while perhaps necessary for our current firm and even for the next generation of the real estate industry, is not the ideal structure. The optimal solution is an industry of firms led by partnerships consisting of A to Z skilled developers who leverage their expertise into great debates and discussions which provide consistently higher-quality building product for us, as well as our neighborhoods and cities.

This brings us to our most revolutionary concept...

Chapter 6

The 'M' Word

"The mind is not a vessel to be filled, but a fire to be kindled." – Plutarch

We continually reiterate two primary goals in this book. The first is very pragmatic and is simply to restore stability to our current firms. The second, much loftier goal is to restore the greatness of our profession for future generations. It is certainly possible to achieve the former without ever addressing the latter. But why expend all that energy without incorporating the extra 10% that can make us truly great? After all, we are developers. We are creators. We influence the trajectory of our cities for decades to come. So, if there were a way for that influence to amount to 100 buildings instead of 20, why would we ever say no?

If we posed the question, "What is the job of the development firm?" to ourselves or any of our developer friends, or our own employees, or even an entire ULI convention, the answer almost exclusively would be: "to create buildings." If we asked TSORE readers, we might even get more than a few: "We become developers when we choose to marry what is inspirational in life with what is best for the public through the nimble use of our developer toolset," or even, "to enhance the lives and experiences of the community while returning a reasonable profit to our investors."

Those are our revised definitions of developer and of success. But the developer is not the same thing as the development firm, and success is a result, not an embodiment. In order to achieve the greatness that is available to us, we must embrace a new understanding of the organizations we own or lead: The job of the development firm is to create developers, not buildings. The job of the developer is to create buildings. This is why we have said that buildings are a by-product of a superior system of development. The system, the realignment and the overhaul are all designed to create superior developers by teaching them to proficiently understand and perform every aspect of the development process and to marry that acumen with strong values and vision.

We have repeatedly described the modern development firm as a factory for low-grade building product. At the enterprise level, our goal is to turn that factory into a more sophisticated machine, to turn it into a laboratory for learning. The development firm must become a school for development, and the products must be A-Z developers who embody the values and expertise of the greatest parts of our new firm.

Once again, we find ourselves referencing the A-Z developer. The success of our future viability hinges upon individuals who have an acute understanding and respect for each and every part of the development process. This may sound somewhat contradictory, since we just closed the last chapter acknowledging that our current firms, once revised and realigned, may be a collection of SMEs. And that's okay, but only for a generation. If we accept the goal of steering our profession back toward its full potential, then we must have comprehensively trained and skilled leaders at the helm. SMEs can stabilize the industry but can never return it to its glory. Our future leaders must have the expertise to correctly answer each of the questions in the Litmus Test.

When we use the term "sophisticated" as above, we mean that we are tuning up the development machine to have "greatly increased functionality and horsepower." In this case:

1. *Functionality* is derived from a leadership team with more robust skill sets to address and teach development from its most comprehensive perspective.

2. *Horsepower* is generated by building the organization to grow and become self-perpetuating.

The marriage of these two ideas will be evident within the organization's culture. This naturally occurs through many of the tweaks and adjustments we have already discussed and will continue to expand upon. Think of it this way: We are simply rearranging the appendages on Mr. Potatohead, not trying to turn him into a zucchini.

As with establishing a mission statement, our organizations also must adopt a culture statement. While the culture statements will differ based on the particular goals, values and vision of the individual firm, each should begin with the words: "My firm is a school for development." That is our thesis, our call to arms. Sounds simple, right? But as we've seen in previous chapters, it is actually more complicated than it sounds. The difference between the "factory for low-grade buildings" and the "school for development" is one of fundamental focus.

What a shift in focus means for the firm's leadership is that our jobs will have to change, or at least the ways we view them. For years, we have taken pride in understanding dirt, raising capital, timing the markets and guiding project; from now on we must take pride in teaching others to do these things.

So who must we become in order to accomplish this? There is a story in the Bible (Matthew 4:19) in which Jesus was walking along the Sea of Galilee and came across Simon and Andrew. These two brothers were fishermen by trade and were in the process of casting their nets into the sea. When Jesus approached, he said that if they abandoned their work and joined with him, they would no longer be fishermen, but would become "fishers of men."

In the same vein, we contend that achieving the generational greatness and success we describe is contingent upon the development firm ultimately becoming a developer of developers. (Fortunately for developers, the firm's goal is only to capture and train the hearts and minds of our protégés, not necessarily to save their souls.)

Shifting Focus

In the last 90 or so pages, we have challenged ourselves to reconsider our values and goals, to have difficult conversations with our partners, to reignite and refocus our love for our profession and to redefine our concepts of success. Our next task is to establish a new role for ourselves within that construct. There has been so much upheaval as we question our values, goals and structure, but, as we know, chaos breeds opportunity. But keep in mind: The immediate results may not seem revolutionary. This is going to take some faith.

We have already touched on the idea that redesigning our firms as schools for development may be the most traumatic of the entire book. It relies on a re-examination of how we view our roles within our firms and within the profession itself. If we have operated for five or ten or twenty years under the belief that our jobs were simply to make buildings or create returns for our investors, then proposing that we become the deans of our own schools for development may be almost a bridge too far. So from a practical perspective, why is this really so important?

At the micro level, our development university will be expected to deliver three things:

1. Better, more responsive buildings,
2. Organizational scalability through a self-perpetuating structure, and
3. A much greater sphere of influence within the industry.

We've already discussed the first item – and addressed it through the institution of the Litmus Test in chapter 5. The second point, a self-perpetuating structure, is an important quality-of-life issue. It's hard to find a real estate developer who doesn't love his job. Even if we have operated under a myopic and misdirected understanding of our role, it is hard to deny the pleasure we've derived from it. There is a primordial joy that humans feel when they create. As we ferreted-out in our first chapter, a significant part of the American Dream has been the opportunity to exploit that bliss. A spirit of innovation, accepting personal risk and an optimistic perspective are a few of the basic building blocks which are unique to our culture and which facilitate that dream. And as we recall, this structure fosters American Exceptionalism. The real estate developer may be among the purest examples of the American Dream and Exceptionalism. For many of us, the concept of a life without our work would be untenable. But there is more to life than just real estate development.

There are beautiful sites to be seen and adventures to be had all over the world. There is the joy of relaxing with our families. There are spiritual pursuits. There are books to be read, tastes to be had and cultures to be experienced. And all of these endeavors will be potentially missed or neglected if we have created an organization that we cannot trust to operate effectively in our absence. It is not unreasonable for real estate development to be our greatest joy; however it would be a shame for it to be our exclusive one.

What a school for development ensures is that we create an environment in which all of our team members are taught to understand and view their decisions through our teachings, expertise and values. We will be able to trust their abilities because we have purposefully taught them everything they know. This stands in stark contrast to the current environment, in which we just assume our team has picked up a few things along the way. By building a team we can trust, we liberate ourselves from at least a few of the 365 days per year we spend running our firms.

The third issue, an increased sphere of influence, may be the most consequential aspect of making the shift because it speaks directly to our legacies. For as much inherent joy as there is in the act of creation, there is also unmitigated pride in viewing the results of our labors. It's difficult to drive by one of our own buildings without pointing to it and saying to our passenger: "I did that." We know that we summoned the forces of capital, design and construction and directed them to our vision. It is a powerful realization – we built that.

Imagine then that a decade into our new business model, some of our fully trained developers will have left our school for development to start their own firms just as we did. Some will be our local competitors, while others will move to other parts of the country to pursue opportunities. But each one does so with a deeply ingrained understanding, love and respect for each and every aspect of the profession. We will have instilled in them a set of values that will inform every building decision they make. Because of our teachings, they understand how to comprehensively and nimbly manipulate each tool in the developer's box in order to create profitable spaces that contribute to their communities. As they carry on the values and beliefs that we so diligently imparted, our professional legacy increases exponentially.

Challenges

While we're transitioning our firms into development universities, we must operate with the understanding that this shift will require a deep commitment. We cannot be part-time or adjunct professors. As with any intentionally learned behavior, this one will require consistent dedication, self-awareness and honesty. It will also take patience: This will be a journey, a difficult one. We may start off clumsily and occasionally stumble, but we will learn and improve. And finishing this chapter and returning to work tomorrow won't result in us *doing* anything differently. Yet. Initially, we have to contemplate and formulate a plan.

There is a challenge that results from the realization that the highest and best form of the development firm is a school for development is not immediately obvious. The obstacle is not that the shift forces the developer to alter his daily tasks. Nor is it that we do not possess the mental wherewithal to conceive and implement a strategy to make the transition. We are by nature some of the world's most nimble professionals. The challenge is twofold.

First, we have a tangible and deep-seated passion for what we do. We love the attention and the spotlight. We love the power of making our own decisions. We love watching our ideas become articulated in the built form. We love negotiating and closing our deals. We love the profit that comes from our risk and labors. And why wouldn't we? Our jobs happen to be truly heroic and inspirational. When we look in the mirror, we see characters that could have stepped out of an Ayn Rand novel or a WPA propaganda poster. As we have repeatedly declared: We are creators. There is an inherent fear that by changing a fundamental component of our profession, one that nurtures every aspect of our being, that we will potentially lose the love and purpose that drives and motivates us. Frankly, this is not an unreasonable concern.

The second challenge we face is embracing the shift from a sole focus on the acquisition of capital and creation of buildings to the creation of developers. We are replacing ourselves as the focus of our professional lives with someone else: our younger and less experienced employee. At some point, this perspective shift will force a mini-identity crisis, which may sound overblown. The concept of putting others first is not revolutionary. But this is different. Our firm is our man-cave. It is not just a job; it's a place we go to celebrate something that is uniquely about us. Displacing that selfish respite with yet another focus on someone else will be challenging for some.

One of great misconceptions of the past few decades and of the decline of greatness in the industry is that developers are the progeny of institutional bankers. In no small part this stems from the fact that a degree in finance and a few years in banking is the most obvious entryway into the profession. No wonder we think we are banker-esque. While mastering capital flows and manipulation is a key understanding required of us, it is not a trait that guarantees success within a highly functioning firm. The key skill we must possess is the ability to sell. Think of developers as salesmen on steroids.

Unlike a typical salesman at Cisco or Hewlett Packard, however, our stars seem to shine a bit brighter, partly because the products we sell are ourselves and our own achievements. We sell confidence. It's not surprising then that many of us fall prey to believing too much in our own sales pitches. Another distinction between the developer and the traditional salesman is that we risk our own capital. The result is unusually high compensation for us, which feeds our unending spring of self-confidence. Of course, the danger is that this cycle can behave like a funhouse mirror, distorting our views of ourselves. All this leads to the idea of the stereotypical real estate developer.

While the actual personalities of developers span the spectrum from introverts to extroverts, humble to arrogant, and meek to bombastic, we must acknowledge that there are certain prolific commonalities that have perpetuated our stereotype. Both developers and investment bankers have long-established reputations for being self-centered pricks. Ask anyone and they'll tell you that we drink too much scotch, eat too much steak, laugh too loud, divorce our wives at 45 and then marry 25 year olds. Unquestionably, real estate developers are known to suck the marrow from the bones of life; or more pejoratively, we are known for behaving badly.

Is this a universally true (or even fair) caricature? Of course not. But it does occur enough that a stigma exists. In fact, one young writer in Dallas, Katherine Harper, created the most amusingly sardonic personification of the stereotypical developer in "The Life and Times of Cash McMogulson III" series, which follows the adventures of Cash, the thirty-something son of a wealthy and established Dallas real estate developer. Here is an excerpt:

My name is Cash McMogulson III, I don't know you, but you probably know me. You've seen me in Paper City or out at the bar. I didn't notice you --- don't worry. I was probably wearing a blazer. My days are always productive and my nights are always awesome. Did I tell you about last Thursday? No! Shit. Well here it goes, another banner night...

My buddies and I went to Bob's for dinner. We do deals. We eat steaks. I got the filet rare. That's what you order. I didn't eat the carrot. That's gay shit. Anyway, our waitress was hot! I've been seeing this girl, Ashley St. Standard. I mean, she's hot too of course, and even though she's pretty average in the sack and not too smart she was in a good sorority --- the same one as my mom. I don't know where she is tonight. Don't really care, but I'm getting ahead of myself. So Bob's was fucking amazing oh and we totally played credit card Russian roulette. I didn't lose, but I paid for the whole thing anyway. Who the fuck cares who pays, it was practically a business dinner since we talked about all the deals I have going on. I always have deals going on. So do my buddies. So then I looked at my Rolex and it was like 10:30 pm, it's EARLY! My buddy Turner Parkerton was so wasted, he's a closer too. That's why we hang out. So anyway he just broke up with his girlfriend who sucked by the way (I mean if she didn't suck, I'd be dating her) and we wanted to find some really hot tail for him I mean, since I'm seeing that girl.

I told Turner I'd drive, so we all got into my black Tahoe. I mean Tahoes are great that's what guys should have. I'd get an '07 Range Rover, but I don't want to beat it up on my hunting lease. The valet took forever, so I just gave the dude a $20. I don't have time to wait for change. It's just a bunch of ones. That's not even money. We were going to go to Sense and get a table and some bottles of Ketel, but we didn't want some North Dallas chicks throwing themselves at us and drinking off our bottles. I don't touch 972s anyway. So in the car we all decided to go cougar hunting. Best sport in Dallas. You know what a cougar is right?

While the portrayal of Cash is often amusing, it is certainly less than flattering. If we were really being honest, we might admit that we can sometimes see parts of this guy in our own behavior, or at least in the behavior of other developers we know.

So if we *are* that guy, in part or in full, what does it take to bridge the gulf from being the center of our professional world to becoming the deans of our new school for development? As we have already stated, we have to shift much of our self-directed energy outward to our protégés and their professional development. Our efforts need to focus on making someone else's star shine. We'll still own the company that is doing great things. We'll still drive by and brag about the buildings we created. We'll still make lots of money. All of our external characteristics will remain, but internally, we will be focusing on growing and developing our students into the leaders of tomorrow. Sort of like our maxim that great buildings are by-products of a superior system of development, our success is also a by-product of being excellent teachers.

How Do We Do It?

When we think back to our years of our primary and secondary education, or undergraduate work, and maybe even graduate school, there are a few teachers that we will always remember. The number of people who have impacted us from a scholastic perspective is usually no more than a handful. And the thing that made them exceptional was the connection that we shared. That connection was forged because they saw something in us and took a personal interest in our growth, development and success. They cared about us and we reciprocated. So as we now become professors, of course we will need to be patient with our students' lack of knowledge and the occasional silly idea about how things work. We will need to forgive the mistakes they undoubtedly will make along the way. But the most important attribute that we must possess as we embark on this path with our development students is a genuine interest in their growth as people and professionals. Like the teachers that affected our lives in the greatest ways, we will need to become their mentors.

Mentorship

Oh no, not the 'M' word. This is where most of us roll our eyes and think back to B-School and the incessant lectures of professors with too many degrees and too little real-world experience, prattling on about the value of a process they'd likely never led. We all nodded our heads in agreement with the professor, with no intention of ever contemplating the subject again after taking the final. For the most part, that's where we left mentorship. But the thing is, those professors were actually right. Mentorship is the key to higher-quality, self-perpetuating firms.

Then why is mentorship not at the core of every successful corporation out there? Is it because it is much more complicated than simply focusing on our products? Or perhaps because the results are not easily quantifiable on a spreadsheet? Certainly one of the great difficulties with mentorship is that few of us have experienced really good examples of it, and therefore, the best path of implementation is not readily evident. Another challenge is that because mentorship is an interpersonal relationship, it will differ with every application.

What we *do* know are which ingredients we need. We know that mentorship requires a sincere investment in our mentees. It also requires a methodical approach, and the results are not immediately apparent. Sounds like a real estate project, doesn't it?

This book is not the place to provide the road map to being a good mentor. An exhaustive study of the subject could fill a library with texts from ancient Greece though our current times. In fact, the subject was first formally introduced in Homer's "Odyssey" with his bumbling character named Mentor. Throughout the centuries that followed mentorship has played critical roles in the religious disciple training of the Hindu, Buddhist, Christian and Judaic faiths. In Western culture, mentorship has played a critical role in the trades (consider the guild system). In modern society, mentorship has been studied and debated so much that an entire industry has been created around defining and honing it. In fact, an Amazon.com book search of the word "mentor" brings up over 200,000 results.

We each need to seek out the information and methodologies that make the most sense for our individual personalities and then doggedly apply the lessons to our daily lives. That said, some of the lessons we've learned in our own pursuits of becoming excellent mentors include:

1. *Mentorship is about an emotional investment.* Certainly, we
   would never question love and care that we feel for our
   families, our parents or our closest friends. The idea that care
   could be a finite substance would sound ridiculous. Entering
   into a mentoring relationship is an act of extending that care

and thoughtfulness to a new individual. It is also a relationship not to be taken lightly or entered into haphazardly. When we hire or accept a new student into our development school, we must positively answer the question, "Do I want to make the commitment to care about this individual for the next five or more years?" If the answer is no, then either the individual is wrong for hire or it's not the right time to be hiring.

2. *A good mentor gives context to the world.* We all recognize that the greatest part of wisdom comes not from knowing the *what* of a situation, but rather from comprehending the *why* and *how* it's all connected. This understanding allows us to turn data into information. Why gives us context. Why allows us to understand connections, make inferences and apply reason.

Why also takes longer to convey. It is a greater investment in an individual. But when we look back on the influencers in our lives, perhaps the only common trait is that they helped us to understand, rather than just inform.

3. *Mentorship is a reciprocal relationship.* If we imagine mentorship to be a situation where our protégé comes to us once a month and asks for advice that we impart, then we're missing the point. As mentors, we are not just their advisors; we are their coaches, counselors, confidants and friends. In a successful mentoring relationship, we understand that even though we are older and more experienced, we too will grow.

Rather than attempting to dictate how to be a mentor, we would like to share some of our experiences with the mentorship that we received.

[Ross Blaising]

In truth, I have never had a professional mentor. There has never been someone in my career who has taken me under his wing and said, "Ross, I will teach you to be a developer." Furthermore, I have never met an individual who has encompassed all the traits that I would deem necessary to be a capital "D" developer. Instead, my development education is comprised of a series of very diverse observations and experiences in which I have applied real estate, art, history, television, movies and the teachings of great leaders and entrepreneurs to my experience with the built world. To some extent, we all do this. For some reason, the stars aligned early in my life and I recognized that I had certain traits that I believed would lead to success. I have always believed that I could change the world. As such, my search for the components to achieve this has always been a very conscious and deliberate one.

At the early age of 14, I did have a mentorship moment that will stick with me forever. At the time it seemed insignificant, but in retrospect made all the difference in my world. Like many others, I am a product of a 'broken' home.

My parents divorced when I was about two years old. I was fortunate that they valued the effects of a stable family environment. In my case, that resulted in having me go to live with my grandparents. Because I was with my grandparents throughout my most formative years, my parental bond was to them. They provided the love, stability, discipline, and established the sense of morality in me, as is the job of any good parent.

When I was about six, my mother remarried and I moved to Michigan to live with her and my new stepfather, returning to Indiana every other weekend to be with my grandparents. Each bi-weekly return to my home in Michigan on those Sunday evenings was a tear-soaked, gut-wrenching event for all parties; I was inconsolable. After three years of high drama on a non-stop emotional rollercoaster, it was agreed that I could return to live in Indiana; however, I'd have to live with my recently remarried father with whom I had little relationship.

My two-hour commute was reduced to roughly 10 minutes and life was much happier. Of course, my struggle to get home (to my grandparents' house) continued. After all, to an eight-year-old without a driver's license, the difference between a 10-minute and a 90-minute car ride is unsubstantial. Six more years of attempts ended when, at 14, I finally succeeded and was allowed to move back to my grandparents' home.

On my grandparents' property was a large picturesque garden that contained a shaded bench where my grandfather would sit, drink iced tea, read the paper, play with our border collie Ralphie and just relax. Not long after I returned home, my grandfather called me over to sit with him and said 'I am so glad you are home. Things are going to be different for you than they were at your dad's house. There will be no rules here. Dinner is at 6 p.m., and if you are going to be late, you should call your grandmother and let her know. If you are going to be out late at night with your friends, you should tell us where you'll be so that we don't worry. There will be no rules until you show us that you need rules. If there is ever any help that you need or advice on a subject, I am always here for you. If you take my advice and it does not work out, there is no length that I will not go to help you make it right. If, instead, you ask for my advice and don't take it, you are on your own to fix it." In reality, my grandfather would have moved mountains to help me in whatever predicament I'd found myself.

Although I did not understand it at the time, and certainly would not have been able to articulate it, that conversation taught me to weigh both the opportunities and consequences of decisions. It reaffirmed for me that there was a support system that was available when I felt that it was needed. This knowledge gave me the freedom to try things and to make mistakes but encouraged me to make thoughtful decisions and to consider their impact. I was not told that I would be bailed out of situations where poorer decisions were made, but that there was a partner there to help me work through them. To me, this is the goal of mentorship.

I tend to view the task of being a mentor less as conveying knowledge -- although that is certainly involved -- but more so as imparting wisdom. The difference between the two is the mentor's ability to place issues in a context, to turn data into information. True mentorship comes from not simply giving an answer, but from helping to work out a problem. In the same vein as our "fishers of men" reference above, we are all familiar with the Lao Tzu (founder of Taoism) saying: "Give a man a fish; feed him for a day. Teach a man to fish; feed him for a lifetime." As we continue through this book, it will become clear that our purpose is to establish the value of mentorship, create a framework or model that enables it, and a system to methodically apply it.

[Robbie Reese]

To me, mentorship is a very organic process. Its path is uncharted and differs with each application. As such, the process is unrefined, and the approach can be as varied as the personalities and experiences that populate our lives. This is what makes it so hard; you can't automate it. But what you can systemize is your dedication to it. As we've already said, successful mentorship relies on reciprocity, on learning and teaching. But the key to meaningful mentorship is having passion for people and purposefully investing in their lives. Mentorship is about moments, and more importantly, the moments between the moments.

For me, that transformative understanding of mentorship began the day my co-author entered our beleaguered development firm fresh from a series of Boston work-out deals. His approach was direct and his leadership style bordered on dictatorial, but his vision and enthusiasm were breaths of fresh air. I knew that he was different, and the very same qualities that made others bristle intrigued me. I was a young, eager student of the real estate development game and I had unwittingly met my professor.

Our relationship began with a series of casual office conversations and debates on the various aspects of development, the value of 1980s New Wave music, and women. One day, we formally paired together as a team with him as the senior developer and me as the junior. It was with this that our relationship began to evolve into a real mentoring situation. We attended meetings together, and he insisted I be at his side for most of them. (This caused a stir in our organization, as it was more typical that the junior member was in the office making edits, revising budgets and proformas, etc.) After each major meeting, we would go off-site and have lunch or coffee and chat about what just happened.

I was encouraged to ask questions. "Explain this construction detail." "Why do things occur in this order?"

"Why did we put our feet down here, but not there?" Nothing was off limits, and we consumed countless restaurant napkins with sketches and notes. These moments gave context to the world of development, and for me, spreadsheets became spaces, spaces became buildings, and buildings became neighborhoods and cities.

The result of our talks was a deep and binding mutual trust. Thinking back on the series of events, they all suddenly feel orchestrated, though no structured plan was ever in place. We had no specific destination in mind other than to create livable communities and to get better each day.

Of the many moments we shared during these couple years, one remains my favorite. It was a warm spring Sunday morning, and Ross and I had met for a patio brunch in Midtown Atlanta to chat about our previous evenings and soak up any remnants of Saturday night's debauchery that might be hiding in our respective systems. From our seats we could see Robert Stern's Federal Reserve Bank building, and our conversation turned to its façade's simplicity of materials and the interplay between shade and shadow. A reformed architect turned developer, Ross spoke of the building as one would a good friend. As our meal ended and the conversation still had not, Ross said in his animated way, "You know what? There really is a better example. Come with me." We jumped in our cars, traveled north six blocks and parked next to Richard Meier's High Museum of Art. Standing across the street, we talked about modern architecture and Meier's interpretation. We discussed the architect's place in history and his aesthetic, and we compared that building to the structures around it. We discussed what the various materials conveyed. The smooth, white, porcelain-enameled steel panels acted as an ageless skin, and I began to see the complexity and depth that was created by the simple manipulation of light. As we entered the building, I began to understand the soul of architecture. Shuffling past historical treasures from the Louvre, Ross led me through the building and discussed with me the true work of art: the one that housed those French paintings and sculptures. "Professor Blaising" peppered me with questions that challenged my instincts. I had never viewed a building from this perspective and haven't viewed one quite the same since.

Bolstered by this mentorship infusion, my confidence and knowledge grew rapidly and soon I was running my own projects, though the lessons were only beginning. Mentorship, as I would come to learn, is exemplified best when a leader can also follow. George Washington Carver famously said, "How far you go in life depends on you being tender with the young, compassionate with the aged, sympathetic with the striving and tolerant of the weak and the strong. Because someday in life you will have been all of these."

As time has passed, my co-author and I have taken turns leading and following but always trusting in each other's commitment, character and convictions. The relationship has engendered countless new ideas, more than one business venture, and if you are reading this, a book espousing our ideals.

The idea evident from these two examples is actually a subset of our third point above (the reciprocity of mentorship): The best mentoring relationships are both very personal and intimate. You cannot fake caring about and investing in someone else. True mentorship relies on making an open and unselfconscious connection with the mentee. It requires trust and respect from both parties.

Establishing our schools of development begins with aligning the partners of the firm in their goals and vision, so that a cohesive mentoring environment can be achieved. Understanding our responsibilities and opportunities in their broadest terms helps to create a foundation upon which we can rebuild our firms as highly functioning, self-perpetuating entities. And a shift in focusing on our own needs to servicing the needs of others fuels this transformation.

The final component of this plan is to ensure that the physical and legal structure of our organization is designed to facilitate our success.

Chapter 7

Anatomy

"The leg bone's connected to the knee bone, The knee bone's connected to the..." – Dem Bones, author unknown

In each of the previous five chapters, we have discussed issues critical to creating a highly performing real estate development firm. We have purposefully done so without ever addressing the construct into which we will drop our new organization. This is because the last component in this logical order is the organization's structural bucket or business model. Before we were prepared to address the questions related to the legal form, or rather begin the discussions with our attorneys, it was necessary to contemplate the issues regarding core and ancillary values, goals and partnership responsibilities. Clearly, each new firm will be unique to our chosen recipe of ingredients, which includes not only these decisions, but also the issues of product type, geographic region, as well as the scale and quantity of product anticipated. For as uniquely customized as our own structural bucket will be, in truth it will conform in many ways to one of very few permutations.

If we were to obtain a large sampling of development firms, and then analyze their primary structures (abstracted to the point that only the skeletal organizational features were apparent), what we would find is that there would be glaring similarities between them: A fact that is irrespective of region or product type. This is because time and trial and error have evolved the modern real estate development firm into a few prominent typological structures. In other words, decades of evolution have already identified the tallest giraffes.

It is useful to note that when we discuss the typologies, we are only discussing specifically the development group. If the overall organization also includes a management or construction company, etc., a level of structure may exist above (or at the very least 'outside') what we are discussing. For our purposes, the development organization or group is discrete. These constructs can be distilled down into four distinct organizational families; which we name the 'silo,' the 'assembly line,' the 'matrix' and the 'hodge podge.' As we read further, consider the firms in which we've worked and identify the characteristics discussed.

What we will find is that often, smaller and older firms will fit less strictly into an individual genus, whereas larger firms will conform much more regularly. Not surprisingly, this occurs for two reasons:

1. *With scale comes complexity.* The larger firms, with greater pipelines, head-counts and overhead, tend to require much more operational structure and efficiency to function properly. In some ways they require sophistication that smaller, more maverick firms do not.

2. *Evolution occurs naturally.* Smaller firms, especially older ones, were commonly created without long-term intentionality. The real estate development firm is one of the few instances where a significant number of the organizations originated in a

single project, having no vision toward the partnership as an ongoing concern. Because of an ever-increasing scale and capital requirements (especially with redevelopment), this condition becomes increasingly rare.

Each of these situations offers advantages and disadvantages.

1. *Danger.* As a firm evolves or grows, its leadership must balance their approach to its organizational and operation structure. Clearly, growth increases the number of individual tasks to be performed, which necessitates higher head-counts (and often diversity of expertise). Both of these conditions affect the required levels of control and operational oversight and policy. Since these remain dynamic throughout the different phases of its lifecycle, the firm's leadership must be anticipatory of these fluid needs. While over-engineering and under-engineering can be equally detrimental, it is important that the firm's structure evolves in concert with its business plan.

2. *Opportunity.* We have already touched upon one of the great truths about developers, which is that we are the creative artists of the built world. Equally, we have discussed our strong pragmatic job requirements, which include finance and project management. Excellent real estate developers must be highly functioning in both right-brain and left-brain tasks. It is the right-brain focus that can often present challenges for the developer in larger, more corporate environments. As with any

artist, the developers' temperaments may not fit easily into the bank or law firm setting.

Under the profession's current trajectory, the development team increasingly exists as a part of a larger structure, which may include construction, property and asset management, investment, etc. The natural ill-fit between personality and corporate culture that we allude to may not be glaringly visible in our existing firms because they are populated with low-grade project managers (the very problem that we are here to fix). However, as our 'schools for development' move forward and create highly functioning A-Z developers, the mismatch will be increasingly apparent. The firm's leadership should consider having a development team operate as a semi-autonomous studio.

3. *The TSORE Approach.* The concept of the School for Development turns our firms' current structures on their heads. Much of this occurs through the developers' shift in focus that was discussed throughout chapter 6. Once we accept that the primary purpose of our firm is to create developers who create buildings (rather than creating buildings), we find that we simply make different choices. As we work our way through Part II of this book, we will see that the ramifications will affect who and how we hire, how we compensate and how we train. The result will be employees with more evident passion

and broader skill-sets, better buildings and more stable organizations.

Dissection

Even in the profession's dilapidated state, one advantage that developers have from a business model perspective is that, at its most complex, the basic firm functions are actually fairly simple, straightforward and logical. Functionally speaking, there are only three necessary components to a development organization: executive, support and development. These break down something like this:

1. *Executive.* As with any company, the Executive Team will include the C-Suite and Boards of Directors and Advisors (if applicable). Specific to a development firm, there will also be an Investment Committee. The executive team functions to provide leadership, vision and capital. They also make the final determination as to which projects to undertake and invest. Depending on the size of the project pipeline, they will act as a primary liaison between execution and finance. A highly performing executive team also markets the enterprise level capabilities of the firm to the various stakeholders: municipalities, the public, capital markets. The marketing of projects is generally better handled at the development level.

2. *Support.* Support functions include human resources, accounting, marketing, assistant staff and perhaps I.T. Although these functions will interact with the entire organization, from a reporting diagram perspective they will

be more associated with the Executive Team than the Development Team. This does not mean that if an accountant is assigned to a development team for a project or portfolio that they are not responsible to the development partner for that associated work. It is just that their ultimate responsibility rolls up to the CFO. The same is generally true for the remaining support functions.

3. *Development.* The Development Team function comprises all of the activities related to the creation of buildings. These will encompass finding and assembling land, financial modeling, establishing a macro and micro vision for the project, selling that vision internally to the executive team, assisting the executive team in funding the project, managing the design, managing the implementation, marketing the product, leasing or selling it, and often assisting in the final disposition. This is of course what we mean by A-Z development.

In truth, a development firm needs no more complexity – it is actually as simple as that. And for many smaller (local) firms, it needn't grow more complicated. That being said, in order to grow and diversify, many firms will fold in other functions and revenue streams, such as property management, asset management and construction. We must remain cognizant that each of these non-development functions are outside of our discussion here. For our purposes, development is development and construction is construction. We will soon see how commingling necessarily differing corporate cultures and key success factors adds schizophrenia to the equation.

Connectivity

As stated above, we can actually simplify the organizational reporting diagram by combining the Executive and Support functions of the firm and placing them above the Development activities. This is useful because functionally both Support and Development logically connect with the Executive, but not necessarily with each other. They interact, rather than connect. This diagrams accordingly:

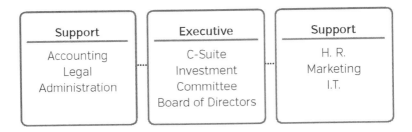

Figure 4. Traditional Executive Organization

With the understanding that the above diagram behaves somewhat monolithically, we can name it the 'executive spine.' From the developer's perspective, it is the remaining relationship (between Executive and Development) that holds the most interest. It is also the executive team's choices around this relationship that give us the best glimpse into the values and vision of the firm's leadership.

At the beginning of the chapter we introduced the four primary structures: Silo, Assembly Line, Matrix and Hodge Podge. Whether we call them typologies or organizational models or structures, what we are describing is the way in which the executive spine interacts with the development team. These typologies are not all created equal, and for as nuanced as they may appear, each comes with drastically varying constraints and implications. Here is generally how they work:

The Silo. The silo organization is perhaps the most traditional of the modern forms of the development firm. Beneath the executive spine a series of development silos exist. Each silo is a self-contained team, which is comprised of a lead developer (perhaps partner) and his supporting development staff.

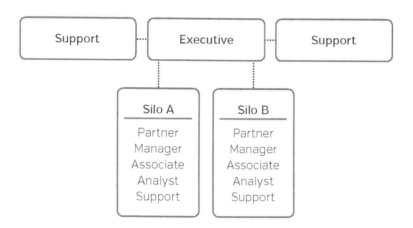

Figure 5. Typical Silo Structure

Advantages. This structure is very stable from a scalability and growth perspective. For firms that engage in more than one type of product or in multiple regions, specialization is also easily segmented. Silos can be added, removed or shifted fairly easily. And where project problems do exist, they can often be contained within the individual silo. The structure is clean and supports entrepreneurship. Employees are easily and logically incentivized for the projects on which they work.

Disadvantages. There are potential problems that can arise with the training of the support staff and the silos sometimes may limit their exposure to various personality types and management styles. Additionally, a partner is an expensive team leader and so this structure can be more costly to operate than others. In smaller firms, partners will commonly inhabit both the Executive and Development roles (keep in mind that these charts represent function more than headcount). Most 'A to Z' developers will favor this type of an organization.

The Assembly Line. The assembly line organization is less common than the silo and often is chosen under three special circumstances:

1. The executives creating the model are not from the development industry. They are likely from fields such as finance, law, construction, the military, or manufacturing. The reason that they are drawn to the model is either that it appears very efficient on paper or that it allows them to reduce the number of highly skilled (and therefore expensive) employees.

2. The firm is located in a region where talented developers are scarce or where it would be difficult to induce them to live.

3. The firm's product is simple and repetitive in nature. There is no vision for growing employees, nor is there a strong belief in them having a long-term tenure. Firms who specialize in rural garden-style apartments, army barracks, or even single-unit retail will be drawn to this form.

Similar to the silo organization, the assembly line begins with the same backbone that contains the C-Suite, Investment Committee and basic services (accounting, legal, human resources) (see Figure 6). The development team layer that is then added has a few leaders who manage the entire process. Instead, a series of functional subject matter experts (SMEs) address their own specific part of the process, and are unconcerned with the entire process. As the project progresses it moves from one team to the next.

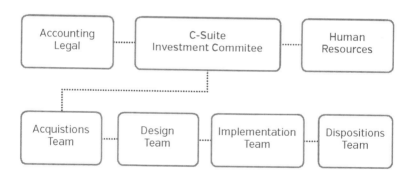

Figure 6. Typical Assembly Line Structure

1. *Advantages.* This is a very owner-centric model. As we've previously alluded, the advantage of this is that the leadership of each team does not need to be multi-skilled or even highly skilled. By utilizing lower-skilled employees, the candidate

pool for replacements is cheaper and more abundant and places less risk on the organization.

2. *Disadvantages.* The Assembly Line firm is not designed to scale or solve complex problems. It also will be less competitive in attracting development talent because is fundamentally misunderstands the mindset of the developer. Almost exclusively, young developers intend one day to become seasoned developers. From the employee's perspective, those who seek the necessary training to eventually become autonomous will be seriously disappointed with this structure, as it is not designed to train them ever to be more than project managers or SMEs. They will likely one day learn that their long-term goals have been inhibited, but usually only after a number of years of 'butt chairing' on the assembly line.

The greater risk to an organization that is not designed to address complex development problems is that while they isolate their lower-level employment turnover, they are also less adept at adapting to market changes. So for instance, once the immediate suburbs are sufficiently populated with garden product, the firm must cease to exist, begin traveling further to other markets that are still in need of this product, or rebuild its business model.

The Matrix. The matrix organization is a typology that we work and interact with very often, but rarely see as a developer's structure (see Figure 7). It is more prevalent with our consultants (e.g., architects and designers, accountants, legal practice groups, etc.) where SMEs are arranged, assembled and reassembled to solve greatly varied, specific problems. In a matrix organization, one professional may be working in various roles in three or more projects, but managing none.

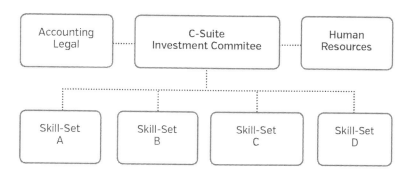

Figure 7. Typical Matrix Structure

As the diagram indicates, a dominant, specific skill-set holder would become the team leader for the project. He would pull together and manage the unique resources, specific to the individual needs of that project. He might lead one project and be a supporting member of multiple others.

Because consulting projects are often quite nuanced, those firms require agility to adapt their efforts to short-term, defined outcomes. And even though every real estate development project is unique, the process and components of the project are generally similar (for similar product types). Additionally, typical large development project cycles may commonly exist in excess of two or three years. These thrive on stability and a consistent vision, which does not conform well to the matrix structure. Matrixes are generally more dynamic and unstable and do not operate efficiently for greater durations.

1. *Advantages.* The matrix has a very adaptable structure.
2. *Disadvantages.* It is very difficult to establish a consistent mentoring atmosphere using a matrix organization. Also, matrix organizations thrive on multiple, short duration specific projects. Real estate development timelines are typically very long and consistent.

The Hodge Podge. Hodge Podge organizations are far too common in our industry. They tend to occur when the development group is an add-on studio, rather than the primary function of the firm (i.e., a construction company dedicating a few employees to development). The Hodge Podge is often a common result when the firm structure fails to evolve at the same pace as the firm's product or when the firm lacks clear vision and leadership.

Hodge Podges tend to proliferate during periods of economic growth and opportunity. As suggested above, they are commonly born out of an existing real estate-related firm (generally construction) that would like to implement a couple of small side development projects. As an initial step, there is nothing wrong with this of course. Structural difficulties arise however if the organization's goal of 'a few small projects' expands into projects of greater quantity and size or complexity.

In this case the challenge comes if the parent company attempts to model the development group in its own form (construction, design or engineering). For example, you simply cannot apply enough Band-Aids to a matrix organization, or the more authoritarian structure of a construction firm, to make it effectively produce high-quality product. As described above, the personalities, skills and motivations are just too different.

Development firms are unique in the way they operate. An easy way to think of it is that 'A to Z' development is a pie with many slices. The developer owns, controls and guides each of those slices. A Hodge Podge often forms when one of the slices (consultants) wants to become the entire pie. Because the business model of most slices is either a matrix (consultant) or an assembly line (contractor), the new development firm replicates that form.

1. *Advantages.* There really are none.

2. *Disadvantages.* It is impossible for the entire pie to exist for long (or certainly not successfully) underneath an individual slice. Even if it could be made to work, it is very schizophrenic. Additionally, the executive mindset is misaligned. After all, how often do executives hire talent to work below them who will necessarily be their boss? Hodge Podge organizations come in multiple shapes and sizes, none of them good.

TSORE Structure

Throughout the book, we have continually returned to the point that the TSORE methodology is intended to refocus our efforts (definitely views, and sometimes actions) by 10% to 20%. In many cases this is as simple as stopping and remembering why we entered the profession in the first place. In others we are asking ourselves to redefine those things in which we have believed, and then to find ways within our structures and partnerships to realign these values within our organizations. And in yet others, we propose concepts that may not have been contemplated previously. We recognize that some firms will require only tweaks, while others may need a complete overhaul.

At the end of the day, we may likely find ourselves making different development decisions. Or at the very least we will make the same decisions, but for different reasons. The exploration and chaos thus far has been mostly internal and theoretical. Rebuilding our organizations is the logical result of rebuilding ourselves.

So when we consider which of the four structural typologies works best for a TSORE organization, what we find is that the Silo is actually the most conducive to meeting our goals. This is for a few basic reasons:

1. *Traditional Structure.* The Silo structure is a traditional organizational typology that is both clearly understandable and also scalable in its form. It works because a single or multiple developers may operate under a supporting spine of services (accounting, human resources, executive functions, etc.). It is compositionally both efficient and malleable. The simplicity of the Silo's form allows it to expand and contract without overhaul.

2. *Fosters Mentorship.* Hopefully by now, the theme is clear that saving the industry relies on the developer retaking his former glory by once again embodying those A-Z skills of previous

generations. By allowing young developers to work on projects from beginning to end, under a single senior developer, they experience the varying complexities that are inherent to each part of a project's lifecycle. The young developer also has the opportunity to see how an individual applies a single value-set to multiple challenges. From the senior developer's perspective, they have the opportunity to engage and mentor the young developer at a much deeper level and for greater periods of time. They have the opportunity to make a significant impact on the individual.

3. *Logical Compensatory Structure.* Because the act of development is very entrepreneurial, the Silo fosters an environment in which compensation may remain segregated and logical. The executive team may easily retain an 'eat what you kill' structure or an enterprise-wide, shared compensation structure without a lot of mental gymnastics.

Conclusion

"In theory there is no difference between theory and practice. In practice there is." – Yogi Berra

So now, as we complete the first part of the book, we are about to leave the theoretical realm. Over the past seven chapters, we have attempted to prepare ourselves mentally for the challenges that our industry faces. The values and vision that we have discussed are only consequential if they are practically implementable. So now we embark on the journey of how to reestablish our firms as the Schools for Development that they deserve to be.

Chapter 8

Tectonics

'If I had eight hours to chop down a tree, I'd spend six hours sharpening my axe.' – Abraham Lincoln

Part I of *The Soul of Real Estate* has been an exercise in illustrating a problem within our industry, defining new goals for success and describing various shifts in our perspective that will aid in the goal of saving our profession. Using Lincoln's analogy, thus far we have only selected the tree. Moving forward, it's time to sharpen the ax. In other words, we must prepare ourselves to perform under a new paradigm.

Having made the decision to become 'schools for development,' we should have already done a few key things:

1. We have spoken with our partners and reached a whole-hearted consensus that TSORE is the path in which each partner is willing to commit their efforts. If the commitment is not unanimous, then the effort is less likely to succeed. We must remember that the change from primarily making buildings to primarily making developers is a seminal shift of mindset. It is a new way of viewing the world.

2. We have defined a core set of values for the firm. These begin with the three universal values of the firm:

   a. Selecting investments that serve their investors.

   b. Developing assets that contribute to the long-term betterment of the community in which they reside.

   c. Structuring an organization that self-perpetuates through sound business practices and strategies.

     And of course, following the universal values are the many unique values chosen by each executive team.

3. We have agreed to an overall vision for the firm. We have considered the product in which we intend to build and invest; where we intend to invest and how we intend to grow and scale. We have also given consideration to ensure that each vision meets the three I's:

   a. The values must be identifiable.

   b. The values must be inspirational.

   c. The values must be implementable.

4. We have created a basic Litmus Test for each new project that we undertake. After developing and customizing our Litmus Test to our unique values and vision, we have looked at the skills of our leadership team and are comfortable that we possess the skills to adequately answer each question in that test. If there is duplication or holes within the team, we have committed to adjusting the leadership team accordingly.

5. We have analyzed the physical structure of the firm, and are comfortable that it is conducive both to fostering the mentorship structure that is fundamental to the success of a school for development, as well as our long-term vision for growth and scalability.

With all of these items thoroughly debated and resolved within the core executive team, this may be the first time in years (or for that matter, the first time ever) that there has been this level of strategic alignment among the firm's leadership. Hopefully the synergies created during this process have also unearthed a new and vibrant energy and optimistic outlook for the future of the firm. For what comes next, we are going to need it.

Focus

As we progress forward, a new term is going to enter our lexicon. Quite regularly, we will discuss and refer to our focus as either 'inward' or 'outward.' These concepts were first introduced on our chapter on mentorship and are key components to our success in establishing and operating our development university.

As with Cash McMogulson, throughout much of our careers our focus with regards to development has been inward. We have chosen projects to meet our needs. We have done deals simply for our own enrichment, and that of our investors. We have hired employees to fill immediate needs within our organizations. We have trained them to fill other needs as they arise, without necessarily considering their long-term career paths, or focusing on the fact that one day they will be making decisions that will affect us, our neighborhoods and local economies.

Although not with malicious intent, the fact remains that we have been greedy. That is an inward focus.

The inward focus may best be summed up by the famous 'Greed is Good' speech from Oliver Stone's 1987 movie Wall Street.

> The point is, ladies and gentleman, that greed, for lack of a better word, is good. Greed is right, greed works. Greed

clarifies, cuts through, and captures the essence of the evolutionary spirit. Greed, in all of its forms; greed for life, for money, for love, knowledge has marked the upward surge of mankind.

Without question there is something fundamentally appealing about this rhetoric. It reinforces the idea that we all have somewhere deep inside of us that we are masters of the universe. It plays to our image of ourselves as the artists and creators which we all believe ourselves to be. Where trouble enters paradise is with what these words do not do. They do not liberate us from our responsibilities to our existing community; nor to the generations to come. In fact, the responsible take-away from the greed is good speech is that we, with all of the gifts that we have obtained, hold a greater incumbency to guide and protect our neighborhoods and cities.

The outward focus removes us from the perspective in which we are the center of our universe. The outward focus recognizes a greater connectivity with our neighbors and customers. It requires us to view our accountabilities from a higher level in which we must consider the needs of those whom we serve. The outward focus is also an acknowledgement that we are in fact, in service to others. The outward focus is an expansive view of the world with a long timeline, whereas the inward focus is myopic and immediate. With an outward view, we recognize that by solving the problems of others, we naturally solve our own. We see that the wealth we generate is not the goal, but rather is a byproduct or an award for the successes that we achieve. With an outward focus we are still greedy, but our greed is tempered with the wisdom that protects and guides ourselves, our families and friends, and the communities in which we operate.

And so it is with these components and these mindsets that we move forward and establish the methodologies under which a school for development will be established. Now we begin to sharpen our ax.

Chapter 9

Mad Men

"What you call 'love' was invented by guys like me. To sell Nylons." – Don Draper

In our previous discussion of necessary skills that a developer must possess, we depicted the developer as 'master salesman.' We painted the image of a confident, charismatic master of his domain. And not without cause. A good developer can work a room of investment bankers, wow a neighborhood council, placate a mob of angry abutters and close the pretty girl at the bar, all in the same night.

Yet, when it comes to the physical marketing of our firms, the developer is lost in the jungle. Sure, our targeted investor packets are concise and superb, as is our project collateral, but when we size up the materials we have to market our actual firms, they're often totally pointless. The problem is that we have content but no strategy. In fact, have you ever wondered why your development firm even *has* a corporate website? Unfortunately, it's probably because your competitors have one, prompting your firm to follow suit. When it comes to general marketing, we all behave like dogs incessantly chasing our own tails. We are broken palindromes: 'I lemming I.'

Think of it this way: A website is a marketing tool, but development firms don't really need to market to anyone (except in specifically targeted, surgical and generally private manners). It's highly unlikely that a major insurance company or Wall Street investment firm is going to call and say, "Hey, I just came across your website and would love to give you $20 million for your next project." Nor do we typically need the public to know who we are.

And yet we all have websites.

There is a famous phrase in the practice of law: "Never ask a witness a question that you don't already know the answer to." But almost every development firm has a website and marketing collateral that answers questions that no one is asking. Because we don't sell a product, our websites merely tend to spout irrelevancies to no one in particular. They just offer up some uninspired corporate-speak such as "Our employees are our number one asset," and of course, an obligatory nod to creating shareholder value. These websites contain pictures of buildings and stock photos of people in construction helmets (so you know that we're professional). There are the firm's Bios section and the Contact Us section for vendors and angry neighbors. But if we were to shut down our current websites, would it impact our businesses at all?

Because marketing a development firm to the general public is virtually unnecessary, our great challenge when attempting to do so is that we lack both a clear purpose (what we want to say) and a defined audience (who we want to say it to). Any marketing or PR professional worth his salt would agree that we're ignoring two of the most basic aspects of strong communications. This lack of direction results in the inept mish-mash of inconsequential data and pictures that we vomit into cyberspace. That is of course, until now.

159

The Soul of Real Estate methodology of vision-led organizations and the School for Development provide the impetus for the marketing of the firm.

Purpose-Driven Marketing

Although seemingly complex with multi-layered tasks and processes, our traditional development firm is actually a fairly simple machine: We buy. We build. We sell. Wash. Rinse. Repeat. And while the steps may overlap, each one involves distinct stakeholders to which only targeted marketing may apply.

1. *We Buy.* The buy phase of a project typically consists of working with brokers or landowners, local neighborhoods and municipalities, and debt and equity partners. Although each of these stakeholders comes to the project from very different perspectives, their concerns are exactly the same: "Can you competently complete the project?" And while the messaging is the same, the marketing to each is specific, unique and discrete. Because of this uniqueness, general marketing strategies are inapplicable.

2. *We Build.* The build phase of a project involves maintenance marketing. New, marketed-to stakeholders are not generally introduced here; rather minor work is involved in keeping the existing team apprised and energized. Additionally, work begins on marketing messaging and collateral for the sell phase, and it is also extremely common that the project is marketed for sale or lease prior to the building's completion.

So the build phase has no unique audience, nor any applicable marketing efforts.

3. *We Sell.* The sell phase of a project likely involves leasing or unit sales activity, and therefore, if there is a consumer component, this is where we see the most obvious form of traditional, public (to consumers) or semi-public (to investors) marketing. If the developer is a merchant developer (intending to sell, rather than own and operate the asset), consideration is also given to divesting all or part of the asset, so simultaneous marketing efforts may be underway with investors, insurance companies or brokers. Yet again, there is no mandate for a marketing strategy that targets the general public, nor a brand for the development firm itself.

Within this traditional cycle, the developer's marketing remains project-focused, so there is clearly little need for our firms to have their own formal branding strategy. In fact, because development firms are primarily looking for lucrative investments that may consist of many considerably varied product forms, the creation of a cohesive brand is difficult. Consider this. We know Hilton as a great and prolific operator of hotels, not as a great developer of them. While they may do both, only one has aspect of their business has a brand because only one is consequential to the public.

That said, a few developers have taken the perspective that their company's product(s) is so consistent and represents a greater and loftier concept such that becoming a brand is both feasible and necessary. Undoubtedly, the pinnacle of development firm brands is the Trump Organization (and perhaps more specifically the branding of The Donald himself). In the case of Trump, the brand is luxury. And the general theme of luxury allows for diversification well outside of the realm of building (i.e. Trump Vodka, the Miss America Pageant, etc.). Other than acknowledging that the model exists, we won't spend our pages here marketing for the Trump Organization; they seem to do well enough on their own.

The business model on which most development firms will concentrate will be limited to the business of real estate development. And so that is our focus.

Development University

The TSORE model alters our general marketing calculus. Clearly, our very targeted, project-centric marketing efforts for equity partners, brokers, and other stakeholders will remain the same, or at least similar. These groups will continue to require exposition and metrics that are specific to their lenses. 'General' marketing will be the marketing of 'us' and will include our firms' websites and any collateral whose subject would be the firm itself rather than a project. This is our opportunity to share the values and vision upon which our firm is built.

TSORE has expended much effort discovering or clarifying our beliefs – as a firm – into cogent and implementable ideas. Many are worth sharing and are certainly more interesting than lobbing banalities about shareholder value. Still, recognizing that we have a valuable message to share doesn't address the entire problem: We do not have a logical audience. After all, a potential general contractor, corporate recruiter or copy machine vendor could care less about our core values or mission. They want a meeting to pitch us their ideas and hopefully end up with a contract. Remember that, for the most part, these people make up the bulk of our website traffic. And frankly, a LinkedIn account has enough information to satiate their needs.

However, another group of people visits our websites: job seekers. Currently, their needs are recognized on our sites through the Employment Opportunities link. Of all of our online visitors, the job seeker is the only one who actually cares about what we value. The unexploited opportunity that materializes in the transition from 'traditional development firm' to 'School for Development' is a clearly defined audience to whom we can market the organization. This shift in audience alone instantly transforms our firm website into our first, best opportunity to explain to those who care exactly what we believe in and what they can expect from us. Just like a traditional university, our website is a recruiting tool targeted at potential and prospective students.

Nut and Bolts

Changing our audience, the message and the purpose of the website content should also precipitate a considerable change in the site's physical form. Much of our previous content will either now be irrelevant, pushed to the background or completely rewritten. In the past, our content was intended to passively inform a general public. Now it must be designed to inspire a specific audience and facilitate a call to action: applying for admission into our School.

So what must change? The answer is our tone, focus and depth of content.

1. *Tone.* Because the typical developer's website does not have a logical audience, there is very little tone consistency across the industry. Not surprisingly, larger firms appear more corporate and professional, while medium to smaller firm websites tend to have more character and run the gamut from boastful to fun to sincere. There's never really been a right or a wrong.

   Tone now becomes crucial because our website is attempting to speak to someone who is not 'us.' Although we have not yet defined the criteria of our ideal candidates for entrance into our University (we will shortly), recognition that they will differ both generationally and experientially tells us that they will be best reached in different ways. And while we will be looking for personalities and skill-sets that will be compatible with the values and vision of our firm, there remains significant distinction between them and us. The following chapters will help to inform the understanding of who our target audience is and how to reach it.

2. *Focus.* This is the first of many times throughout the second part of TSORE that we'll highlight the major shift from an outward to inward focus. Because we've redefined the purpose of our development university website in order to entice highly qualified candidates, we cannot achieve this by simply telling people why we are excited about ourselves.

Of course they need to know what we believe in, but they also need to know what we are going to do for them. The application/admissions process is reciprocal, and we can't choose the best candidates if the best candidates never apply. Remember, they are coming to us to learn, and so they need to be confident that we are the best teachers. Otherwise, they can just as easily go to a non-TSORE firm and sit in their windowless office, running spreadsheets for two years, hoping to pick up some additional knowledge so that one day they can become average project managers and perhaps even butt-chair their ways into getting more important titles.

The candidates that come to TSORE firms don't want to gamble with that path. These kids want to be real developers, and they need to know that our firms are different. They need to know that we are here to guide and mentor them.

3. *Content.* This is where the creation of a website becomes fun. Whether we choose to invest $2,500 or $20,000 into its development, for the first time we have the opportunity to actually say something of consequence to someone who wants to hear it. Of course, each of our websites will be as unique as our individual firm. However, there are certain overarching points that will be consistent among TSORE firms:

- Some of the new content will address our real, newly articulated values.
- We may discuss the vision for our firm and our School for Development.
- Significant parts of our curriculum should be displayed.
- We will highlight our commitments to them and our expectations of them.
- We will post our very specific application guidelines and instructions.

Naturally, the websites will include our executive team bios, contact information and some project examples. For firms with more technologically focused leadership, a blog may become a component.

We have the opportunity to build both purposeful and deeply personal websites. One of the keys to successfully marketing our own development university is ensuring consistency among the conveyance of firm values, what its goals are and how it achieves them. As with mentorship, one strategic move that will serve us well here is to abandon self-consciousness in our approach. A sincere statement of real values will inspire our target audience much more than a bunch of MBA-speak.

Chapter 10

The Laws of Attraction

"What you seek is seeking you." – Rumi

The ultimate success factor in becoming a functioning TSORE firm relies on an effort not previously contemplated by industry leaders: attracting talent for our school. Of course, we have interviewed multiple candidates for open positions. We have hired recruiters to scan the marketplace for specific skill sets. We likely even have a drawer somewhere that contains a stack of unsolicited resumes.

But what we are about to undertake is different. After we do this, never again will we consider hiring a recruiter to fill a position on our development team. A substantial part of this shift and its implications is that we are no longer trying to attract developers who are looking for a job; instead we want the brightest young professionals who seek an education and are willing to invest years of their lives with us pursuing it. Sounds daunting, right?

While the many steps in our journey to building a better firm are not necessarily individually difficult, we know from experience that the greatest impediment is the psychological shift toward first valuing the proposed change, and then agreeing to undertake it. This is why so much effort was spent in chapter 9 to convince us to transform our corporate website from a flaccid billboard into a performing marketing tool directed at our target customer (the student or future employee). We chose to highlight that particular medium, not because the website has an inherent value which towers above the rest, but because the website exemplifies an investment in both time and capital that offers us no potential return. When we posit that our challenge is psychological in nature, reflect again upon the subject matter of chapter 8: The shift in focus is from "us" to "them."

Before we alienate the entire recruiting industry (hopefully, they don't possess a strong lobby in Washington) by stating that we no longer require their services, we should be clear that we are not talking about changing our hiring practices for every position in the firm. Specifically, we are referring to the development roles. The criteria for hiring accountants, secretaries and other similar roles can remain as is typical for their part of the industry. One major change regarding the acquisition of young developers-to-be requires that we recognize that our education is most effective when received entirely within our school. And students with no experience don't require recruiters.

Accordingly, we must place tremendous focus on the approach we take when hiring (admitting) developers: How do we evaluate and choose between candidates? What criteria should be considered? Is there a new or different process or method to employ?

Let's start with that shift from us to them and ask ourselves a simple question: Why would *they* want to work for *us*? From the outset we must recognize that we're not doing these kids any favors by taking them under our wings. These folks that you want for your team – they have other options. So again, ask yourself: 'What do I offer that makes *me* a compelling choice for *them*?' SPOILER ALERT: It isn't money.

Before we even begin to think about evaluation strategies or interview processes, let's start with a very basic question: 'What is the candidate's psychology?' Think back to your early Developer Days. Consider the unending spring of self-confidence that drove you here, to the now. Think of the fortitude necessary to take the risks you've taken throughout your career, and recognize the role that luck – and eventually wisdom – played in the mix. Remember how many times you were chided for 'wanting too much too soon,' or for 'constantly over-reaching your experience-level,' or told that you need to 'tone it down a bit' to fit into the corporate culture. You knew from day one that you were destined for greater things.

Your path was inevitable. You didn't have a choice and neither do the guys you want on your team. The thing to recognize is that great leaders and entrepreneurs are born, not manufactured. We are the Yodas to these young Luke Skywalkers. The best we can do is hone the natural talents and gifts they've been given or have crafted with help from parents, schools, churches and communities, as well as adversity. In their mid-twenties, they're blank slates – except when it comes to development.

We just acknowledged a realization that we'll flesh out later: that 'Gordon Gecko, Master of the Universe' personality we all share? It was perpetuated, at some point, within each of our individual educations and journeys. Perhaps it was a Bilbo Baggins-type story in which fate and circumstance collide, such that we rise to the occasion as the reluctant heroes. Or maybe it's the Atticus Finch storyline, where our moral codes and archetypal views of manhood dictate that being anything but a hero is untenable.

As the deans of our own schools for development, our process must identify the qualities of a heroic leader. Unquestionably, science is on our side. How often do we see the same personality type at the helm of organizations? Why is the heroic visionary so necessary to a firm's success? And more importantly, at what point in a leader's career do they become the larger than-life-visionary?

Our firms' answers to these questions identify the bull's-eye of ideal candidates for our school. And a defined methodology creates a strategy to evaluate them. These are undoubtedly lofty goals for an interview process. But if achieved, all of our sluicing efforts through the riverbeds of potential talent will identify the shiny nuggets we seek. Our efforts will pan out.

Positioning the Firm

When considering the seasoned developers reading this book, we can imagine the numerous distinctions they will find between their current experience and the principles and methods we espouse. This is especially true if that experience is with a large corporate firm. In that case, do not mistake size or funding for success. It is equally possible for a very large firm to positively contribute to or negatively erode the quality of our cities and the talents of those making decisions in our firms. In general, we discuss the development firm as an autonomous unit, but rarely differentiate whether that unit is the entirety of a small firm or a studio within a much larger organism.

The importance of the discussion on the personality of a developer becomes clear when viewed against the backdrop of the large factory-for-building-product model versus the small, nimble development firm. Of course, there are various advantages and disadvantages to each typology. And certainly, the constraints of funding and influence associated with smaller firms will often make the large-firm route seem more appealing. But one of the greatest challenges for the heroic A-Z developers we are trying to create and mass produce is the dichotomy between the natural personality of a charismatic leader and the necessary goals of the large organization.

The problem, of course, is that the large firm, in seeking stability, rejects the potential chaos that can result from substantial, and sometimes competing, egos. Those of us who matriculated through one of these behemoths can likely remember the years of frustration we felt as we attempted to fit into someone else's box of 'appropriate.' The TSORE organization, on the other hand, embraces this energy. Rather than begrudgingly apologizing for our teams' cult of personality, we seek these type of people out, admit them to our programs and train them to hone their egos to their advantage.

So the question remains, can a school for development operate and thrive under a large umbrella? We believe that the answer remains yes, but that it will be more difficult and will require some modifications. The key is to understand that any diversely skilled set of companies that are intrinsically linked together must still be allowed to operate individually. We must continue to recognize that the individual vertebrae of our corporate spine may have a different shape and fit together in very different ways.

While property management, construction, capital and acquisitions can easily be ordered within their own individual, neatly-shaped boxes, we may find instead that the development group is more properly contained within a bag. This comes from that recognition that the personalities and talents we are taming are simply unique. Each young developer will have a slightly different method that brings out their best work, and for our mentorship model to work we will need to adapt a structure that allows for that to occur.

In an interview from the Pierre Berton Show in December 1971, Bruce Lee aptly described the fluidity needed to be a Kung Fu master: "Empty your mind, be formless. Shapeless, like water. If you put water into a cup, it becomes the cup. You put water into a bottle and it becomes the bottle. You put it in a teapot it becomes the teapot. Now, water can flow or it can crash. Be water, my friend."

In his case, Bruce was describing an approach to a martial arts battle, but the premise applies to our development businesses as well. When large companies seek stability, they will typically dumb down their development talent with personalities that fit their predetermined box. THIS IS THE WRONG SOLUTION. Development teams are necessarily small and very entrepreneurial. Even within the constructs of a larger umbrella, the TSORE development team needs to be a more autonomous group with a different set of rules. It may even be best to house the developers in their own space, away from the more standardized functions.

Changing Course

For decades now, development firms have hired the wrong people for the wrong reasons, and then have not comprehensively trained them. If we intend to dedicate ourselves to making smarter development decisions and creating a higher standard of excellence within our firms, it is time to break this dysfunctional cycle. In a brilliant comedic exchange in Whit Stillman's 1994 movie *Barcelona*, the lead character Ted Boynton, a US Navy officer stationed in Barcelona, is lying in bed with his Spanish love interest Marta (a local trade show beauty) after an evening at the disco. Ted ponders aloud to Marta:

> "Tonight, while shaving...I always shave against the beard for a closer shave...I remembered this razor ad on TV showing the hair follicles, like this. The first of the twin blades cuts them here," he says, motioning downward against his left cheek. "Then the hair snaps back and the second blade cuts them here...for a closer, cleaner shave. That we know.

> "But what struck me was: If the hair follicles are going in this direction and the razor is too...then they're shaving in the direction of the beard, not against it.

> "So I've shaved the wrong way all my life. Maybe I misremembered the ad. The point is...I could've shaved the wrong way all my life and never have known it. Then I could have taught my son to shave the wrong way, too."

> "You have a son?" queried Marta.

"No…But I might someday. Then, maybe I'll teach him to shave the wrong way."

"I think maybe my English is not so good."

It will be impossible for us to restore consistent excellence to the profession until we make better hiring decisions, based on different criteria and followed with a defined training curriculum. We need to teach these kids to shave the right way.

For much of the Industry, the hiring strategies for real estate developers are very similar, if not the same. Firms are initially drawn to candidates with two or three years' experience in banking and/or consulting. Because their first job will be as an Analyst, the primary skill required is the ability to learn and run a proforma. Eventually, they will work on assembling ownership reports, periodic re-forecasting and other financial analyses. After a couple of years, they will be promoted to a Development Associate position, taking on slightly more responsibility, and finally, to Development Manager, a role that amounts simply to project management. A very few will progress to a Partner or Development Director or Vice President level position.

No wonder our buildings and streetscapes are becoming increasingly atrocious. The ante into our organizations is a simply taught 'hard skill,' followed by anecdotal learning, rather than intentional, comprehensive training. We are giving our youth a spreadsheet and telling them that they are now developers! This is simply absurd.

So what is the right solution? The initial answer is simple: Stop hiring for hard skills. That is a 'fill the hole' mentality, which reflects tactical decision-making. 'Filling the hole' would include hiring for a particular skill when there is a capacity need within the organization. Suppose we are analyzing a number of potential projects, so we hire an analyst to fill the hole.

This is not an effective long-term approach. Every hire to the team needs to be a long-term commitment and should have the aptitude necessary to eventually become a partner. Doing this would indicate and encourage a shift to making consistently strategic decisions, rather than tactical ones. Hard skills include:

- Financial analysis
- Knowledge of Excel, Argus or any other computer operating system
- Project management designations, such as PMP
- Any other skill that is easily taught or stand-alone in its use

What happens when we lose an employee during training and need that skill immediately? Again, there is a very simple answer: Every hire is strategic and long-term. If we find that we need an analyst in the short term, or a project manager, then we should hire a contractor. Buy a toolbox, rent a tool. Financial analysis, for instance, simply involves a hammer. Don't have a particular hammer? Rent it.

And so we return to this chapter's original question: Why should candidates choose our firm? Because we are viewing the world from their perspective instead of ours, because we are no longer hiring them for a simply taught hard skill, and because we are committing to an investment in their talent, the answer is again, quite simple. If you can tell them, "The value proposition that my organization offers you is that after six years with me, you will be a developer. Because of my structure and program, in a little more than half a decade you will be my partner, or you can leave me and be qualified to be a partner at any company in the country, or you will have the tools to start your own firm – if you can raise the talent and capital to do so. Mine is a school for development."

This is all you have to say, and it is all they want to hear. Remember, these candidates are confident in their potential and their aptitudes. They believe that they know their destiny. In fact, when they look at you, they think that they are you – only younger. You can pay them less and work them harder if you can deliver on that one single promise. But you must be able to deliver, which is everything this book is about.

Chapter 11

Size Matters

"Step 1. You get a box.
Step 2. You put a hole in the box.
Step 3. You..." – Justin Timberlake

With each chapter, we progress toward the eventual process of hiring (accepting) our young students and future developers. Because we have agreed that each new hire is strategic, and we are viewing the mentoring commitment as a six to seven year endeavor, it is now even more incumbent upon us to get that hiring decision right. And so it should not come as a surprise that a TSORE firm will view this process slightly differently than our traditional counterparts. As we said in chapter 3, 'For years now, we have hired the wrong people for the wrong reasons and not comprehensively trained them.'

The contrast will be palpable when we simply contrast the TSORE proposition with our own experiences rising through the industry. When we were initially hired, most of us had a connection into the industry, a specific skill that was lacking in the firm or a finance background. In any situation, we also likely had a story that was directly relatable to the hiring manager. Regardless of the specific firm or manager, it is a generally observable truth that individual leaders and managers typically value the skills that they possess more than the skills in which they are deficient. Accordingly, they also value their career path over other alternatives.

After all, it is their skills and path that brought them to the point where they are now in the position to evaluate others.

This prejudice becomes most apparent when hiring more seasoned employees for senior positions. For instance, if we came up through the industry from the construction side we would likely have the ingrained tendency to believe that the real differentiating quality for a developer is an understanding of how the building goes together. Or if we began our career as a banker, then an intimate understanding of capital flows may be our hot button.

These preconceptions often lead to one-sided hiring decisions. As we have seen, a strong component in the progressive degradation of our profession has been the result of this way of thinking. The developer is not one or even three things. The *Developer* must truly be a renaissance professional. This means that he masters a dozen proficiencies and is nimble enough to perfectly juggle them through multiple projects' very kinetic lifecycles.

Capacity and Likelihood

Throughout the book we have referenced the 'toolbox,' and have recently alluded to the concept of toolbox hiring. What we have not done is describe what a toolbox actually is, and differentiate it from a tool. The simplest way of distinguishing these two components is to view the toolbox as representing a person's capacity to succeed at the role of developer, where the tools are the individual skills that they must possess and utilize toward that success. The more tools and the greater the proficiency with them, the greater the likelihood of consistent success. It is useful to note that every profession, career and role has its own unique toolbox and tools upon which success relies. The following paragraphs will discuss both the toolbox necessary for creating A-Z developers, as well as the tools (skills), bifurcating them into hard and soft varietals.

In our example above of typical hiring manager prejudices, the problem illustrated is that long-term human capital investment strategies rely on hard-skills thinking. By ennobling capital flow analysis (an easily taught hard-skill) to a primary driver of the hiring decision, we equate – or worse, elevate – a simply taught skill to or above the individual's capacity to succeed at the breadth of tasks necessary for success. We must understand that our hard-skills have nothing to do with our ultimate success as a leader. And our ability to lead is our ultimate success factor.

THE TOOLBOX. We refer to the 'toolbox' as one's capacity to grasp, process and utilize the tools that we are hoping to develop in our young associates. We have also said that the tools within the toolbox fall into two categories, hard-skills and soft-skills. Additionally, we will see that hard-skills are more easily taught than soft-skills, with the soft-skills being the more complex and important to a person's long-term success. The most complicated however, is the toolbox itself.

As we begin this discussion, we must say that understanding capacity does not necessarily guarantee the success of the associate; nothing does. The best that we can achieve by isolating the toolbox is positioning our hires for the likelihood of success. Freewill and circumstance will always play a role the associate's path.

That said, the toolbox is comprised of two different components: personality and intelligence. Each of these is very complicated and generally too far outside of the expertise of almost every leadership team to quantify on its own. Fortunately, there are tools that we can rely on to inform us of the breadth and depth of the capacities of each of our competing candidates.

Personality. The first step in really understanding the toolbox comes from understanding the candidate's personality. When we refer to personality, we are using the term more in a Jungian sense than necessarily whether they are amiable, etc. 'Personality' from this psychological perspective is focused on quantifying our candidates' rational and irrational functions. This relates to how they judge and how they perceive. From a dimensional perspective, imagine personality to be the length and width of the toolbox, while intelligence is its depth. Together these two elements are its capacity.

If we were to survey the personalities of the C-Suite of most successful, sophisticated companies, there would be certain commonalities among these traits and tendencies. It is easily understandable that there are certain personality types that naturally gravitate toward leadership roles.

The Myers Briggs Foundation, which revolutionized the quantification of personality and type (psychometric analysis) through a series of standardized questionnaires, analyzes four primary aspects of the personality that, when combined, break every human down into 16 basic personalities. Their test also fine-tunes the four personality traits (which they call dichotomies) into a sort of 'low to high' level of influence (scale). For instance, a basic distinction as to whether someone is naturally introverted versus extroverted may be somewhat useful, whereas pinpointing whether they are slightly versus highly introverted or extroverted is certainly more useful.

The better we can understand fundamental aspects of our candidates' personalities,, the clearer picture of an individual we can gain. And while we can all agree that there are these personality commonalities, what is really interesting is how accurate personality testing actually is. For instance, the majority of Fortune 500 CEOs fall into two basic personality types that, when added together, make up less than 4% of the world's population. It is staggering to imagine that 4% of the world's workers are really competing for the most influential jobs in the world.

We may remember a few years back, in 1999, when Jack Welch (the former CEO of General Electric who is often regarded as the greatest CEO of the late 20th century) announced his retirement, that a very visible, public debate occurred as to who would become his successor. The fervor was not surprising; after all General Electric was then the world's second largest company, with a market cap of roughly $505 billion (Microsoft was the largest at the time). As the edict was to promote from within, the competition to helm this behemoth came down to three individuals: Jeffrey Immelt (president and CEO of GE Medical Systems), W. James McNerney Jr. (head of GE Aircraft Engines), and Robert Nardelli (head of GE Power Systems). In the end, Welch and the Board of Directors opted to award the position of CEO to Immelt. Soon thereafter, both McNerney and Nardelli left the company to become CEOs of 3M Company and Home Depot, respectively. Neither leader had specific expertise in either of their new industries, but that was irrelevant. The key success factor for each was leadership ability, which is transferable.

Of the 4% of the population described above, a small number will choose that large-company path; however most will end up as entrepreneurs, of which some will be drawn to leadership roles in smaller organizations, like ours. Of the tens-of-millions of great ideas and innovations that exist worldwide, only a small number are ever attempted and only a much smaller number achieve any level of success. This is in no small part due to the toolbox of those that lead the development and finance and marketing of the idea or product.

Some prominent individuals with one of these two personality types include: Franklin D. Roosevelt, Richard M. Nixon, Al Gore, Margaret Thatcher, Steve Jobs, John F. Kennedy, Thomas Jefferson, General Colin Powell, Donald Rumsfeld, Arnold Schwarzenegger, Michelle Obama, Lance Armstrong, Rudy Giuliani. Our goal is to identify that 4% in our interview process.

Almost every large corporation has come to acknowledge that personality is a key component in the long-term success of an employee. This is why the personality test is a common requirement in so many organizations today. In fact, there exists an entire industry built around dissecting one's personality and comparing it to the norms of a job description. From consultancies as large as the

Gallup Organization to a myriad of small, boutique firms, there are thousands of professionals who dedicate their lives to tailoring surveys and interpreting this personality data in hopes of anticipating an employee's thought process and reactions.

Although our discussion revolves around Myers-Briggs, there are a number of high-quality options to choose from in the personality-testing arena. Our concentration on that system comes from the fact that they pioneered the field and that their test is the most recognizable. But while the Myers-Briggs is also our favorite, other tests may work equally well.

Throughout this book, we have consistently stated that developers have been hiring for the wrong skills and reasons (tactical versus strategic). And as we've repeated many times now, each of our additions to the development team is a strategic hire. We must understand that it is impossible to make that strategic decision without an understanding of the candidate's personality.

That said, when it comes to using the results of the personality test, we mustn't forget that while it is a useful supporting tool, in and of itself it does not give us a robust picture of a candidate, nor does it isolate or quantify the capacity of their toolbox. Personality without intelligence is just a cleaver, not the scalpel that we are trying to identify.

Intelligence. The second major attribute of the toolbox is intelligence. The standard measure of intelligence is the intelligence quotient or I.Q. As we all know from having taken them multiple times in our lives, quantifying intelligence is typically achieved through the administration of an I.Q. Test. Other relevant aptitude tests which concentrate on intelligence (as well as prerequisite knowledge) include the SAT, GMAT or LSAT. And while requiring an I.Q. test as part of the interview process can be as informative as the Myers-Briggs test above, it is not always necessary, and some may opt for the lesser path of comparing the results of the standardized tests listed above.

However, before we acquiesce that intelligence is a key component in one's capacity, let's make sure that we are all on the same page as to how intelligence is defined. The Random House Dictionary defines intelligence as one's "capacity for learning, reasoning, understanding, and similar forms of mental activity; aptitude in grasping truths, relationships, facts, meanings, etc.," and the intelligence quotient as "an intelligence test score that is obtained by dividing mental age by chronological age and multiplying by 100: a score of 100 thus indicates a performance at exactly the normal level for that age group." Note that that means that the I.Q. is not a static number.

It is this performance aspect that is most important to identifying the 'size' of the toolbox. For our purposes performance = speed. Let's think of it this way: Stephen Hawking has been long considered to have the highest identified I.Q. in the world. If it were it possible for us (or anyone) to sit down in a room with Hawking and be simultaneously administered an I.Q. test, at the end of the test we could have each answered every question correctly and received very different I.Q. scores. This comes from the speed with which we are able to derive the correct answers. Spoiler alert: Hawking would have been faster.

Throughout the process of 'making' a building, the real estate developer is tasked with juggling multiple relationships from the various stakeholders: finance, municipal and community concerns, design and construction issues, sales or lease-up, etc. An added level of complexity is derived from the fact that the importance of each of these influences is also in flux throughout the project's lifecycle as it moves from inception to completion. And while there are many obvious connections between the varied parts and pieces, many more remain subtle.

The ability for the developer to understand this interconnectivity and the flux of shifting expansions and contractions of the risk associated with each aspect or phase of a project is a fundamental tool necessary to protect the success of that project, as unforeseeable events will invariably occur through its lengthy lifecycle. This requires a substantial toolbox.

Our efforts in identifying and training developers with robust toolbox capacities will ultimately give us confidence that those who work for us can quickly identify, interpret and form generally 'correct' conclusions from disparate sources of information. As we described above, the most important success factor in development is leadership ability. This acumen relies heavily on the interplay between toolbox and the soft-skills. The second most important success factor for a real estate developer is anticipation, and is a direct descendant of the toolbox (combined with experience and wisdom). Therefore, the most critical components of a successful development career are leading through vision and values, and correctly anticipating opportunities and risks. With some luck, that successful development career is paired with prosperity.

THE TOOLS. By defining the toolbox as specifically personality and intelligence, that leaves a lot of components necessary to good developers as yet unidentified. These new massive grey areas are what we refer to as the tools. Much of the time that we commit to over the next half decade will focus upon developing and honing the tools necessary for the consistent success of our development students.

To reiterate the significance in the shift from the current industry standard of hiring for tools to the TSORE proposition of toolbox hiring, our model actually turns the mentality of talent acquisition on its head. So when we said earlier that each hire is a strategic, long-term commitment rather than a fill-the-hole, tactical short-term commitment, we inherently necessitate a different process for selection with different criteria. We are hiring them for different reasons, making a different commitment and offering them different rewards.

It is the 'offering them different rewards' which delivers us the most stability – because it is what keeps them. Under the traditional system talent retention is aspirational. We hope that our team doesn't abandon us at a critical time in a project. Of course, since they are working on multiple projects at different points of progress, if they do leave it most certainly will be very inconvenient. But we do understand that our employees will leave once they feel that they are either (a) no longer learning, or more likely (b) when a competitor offers them more money. In other words, they will leave when they feel that we no longer offer them something that is unique and compelling. This traditional system abdicates control of stability within our team to our competitors. And through the traditional system of training, we are unwittingly injecting potential chaos into the organization.

Inherently, by shifting our primary focus in the admissions process to the candidates' capacity, we subjugate their learned skills (tools) to, at the very least, a secondary position. In reality, once we bifurcate hard-skills and soft-skills, those are secondary and tertiary positions. Through our hierarchy, we are effectively saying when it comes to skills 'yeah, we can teach that.' And if we already intend on equipping them with these skills they need to succeed during their at least six years under our scholastic wings, then there is also an obvious and significant advantage to hiring young developers-to-be with as little experience as possible (and consequently fewer developed tools). After all, if we truly believe that our competitors are not training their employees appropriately, we will want to limit the amount of time that we spend un-training their bad habits in order to replace them with good ones.

Having fewer or limited skills does, of course, not mean that a candidate comes to us with no developed skills. They are not totally blank canvases. And yes, we will want to quantify and evaluate the skills that they do retain. But we do so with the understanding that tools will almost never be the differentiator between success and failure within the program, whereas capacity assuredly will.

What is the difference between a hard-skill and a soft-skill? If asked, each of us could create a list of soft-skills and hard-skills that when compared side by side would likely be at least 90% similar to anyone else's. An understanding of the types and categorization of these soft-skills certainly does exist in the popular consciousness. However, from the perspective of making the best 'strategic hire' the definition of what one 'is' or which column to place it in, is much less relevant than understanding how they originate or how they figure into one's success. Both hard and soft-skills constitute valuable tools, but for our purposes hard-skills are those that can be more easily taught, where soft-skills are those which must be honed.

Hard-skills are straightforward and logical. They are tools such as calculus, organic chemistry, diagramming a sentence, creating or manipulating a proforma, managing a budget or following the prescriptions of a development cycle. Languages, methodologies and processes are hard-skills.

Soft-skills, on the other hand, are at least semi-embedded in our DNA or formed at a very young age. Some soft-skills include being a compelling or inspirational speaker, having an intuitive sense of proportion or having the mental dexterity to simultaneously view the world from both a ten foot and a ten thousand foot perspective. Charisma is a prime example of a soft-skill.

Without arguing the exactitudes of the 'nature versus nurture' debate, we are generally convinced that people are born with innate aptitudes and personality traits that can later be refined, but not given to those who do not possess them. Further we believe that the process of honing these soft-skills becomes increasingly difficult with age. In part, this is because the soft-skills are more closely associated with the overall toolbox than the hard ones.

It is clear from the two preceding paragraphs that, although distinctly different, hard-skills and soft-skills are mutually reliant. They are also hierarchical. Imagine that a soft-skill is like an electric drill and that hard-skills are like the various drill bits and screw chucks. And while both must work together and both must be present for effective drilling, one is more costly to replace. For instance, if language (words and vocabulary) is a hard-skill and being a compelling speaker (usage) is a soft-skill, the hard-skill must be present to take advantage of the soft-skill. In this example, the soft-skill of being a compelling speaker is a condition of being born with an ability (toolbox capacity) that has been honed by some combination that might include being an avid reader from a young age, early participation in theatre or other form of public performance, growing up in an articulate family, etc.

Thus, by the time that a candidate reaches us, much of this skill is already in place. Our results may be confined to helping 'tighten-up' the skill, perhaps through experiences watching or giving presentations, experience leading meetings, joining a public speaking club (e.g., Toastmasters), assigning a required reading list, etc. But the likelihood that we could drastically affect a soft-skill is significantly diminished and they become much more effort-intensive to cultivate.

The hard-skills such as financial analysis or knowledge of construction methods are considerably easier to train or develop. This is why we have said to generally ignore hard-skills in the candidate evaluation process, and instead to concentrate on really understanding the toolbox and the soft-skills.

Even with an understanding of the definitions and etymologies of hard-skills versus soft-skills, we are still left with a question: What are the key soft-skills that we must identify? As we stated in the introduction of this chapter, all soft-skills are not created equal. It is also true that because each of our organizations has unique value sets and our leadership teams have differing competencies, it would be impossible to create a universally comprehensive list and order of the soft-skills. This is another area that must be customized on an 'organization by organization' basis. As values-based organizations, we must be honest with ourselves as to what we deem to be important. As such, we need to place the additional skills that are important to us on our list and test for them during the interview process.

That said, there are a few soft-skills that should undeniably top the list, and we call these our 'Primary' qualities. Additionally, we suggest some 'Secondary' qualities that we feel are important; however as we have stated, this list is not exhaustive.

Of the qualities that we want to identify and quantify during the application and interview process, the primary three include: (a) verbal skills, (b) a history of success, and (c) the 'get it' factor. In case these do not seem intuitive, let's remember what the role of the developer is in the organization. As we previously described, at our most base level we are salesmen. More specifically, we are salesmen who love buildings. Every aspect of our success relies on our ability to sell our vision: to our organization, our consultants, our debt and equity partners, our neighborhoods and local municipal authorities, and finally the end-user. Everything that we achieve has at its base factor of success, a reliance on our ability as salesmen.

In fact, if we were to go outside onto the street and ask anyone that passed us to name three prominent real estate developers, most couldn't do it. But they could all name one, Donald Trump. No matter what our individual opinion of him or his lifestyle may be, we all know who he is and what he's up to. He is the consummate salesman. The thing to know about The Donald is that his status would have risen in any vertical that he would have chosen because of his toolbox and his soft-skills. For obvious reasons, he chose his family's business. However, if he had instead opted to sell nuclear power stations as a young man, we can all be assured that our landscape would be populated with clean energy production plants today.

Communication skills. In our experience, there is no greater differentiator in the ultimate success of an individual than their communicative dexterity. This quality is almost universal among leaders. Regardless of whether we are naturally extroverted or introverted the ability to convey simple or complex thoughts clearly,

191

concisely and compellingly is irreplaceable in the role of CEO or President or Development Partner; it is also the instrumental trait in getting us there. It is the yardstick by which we are all measured.

As was exhaustively discussed in chapter 3, leadership is comprised of two primary components: values and vision. We live and operate under a guiding set of values and we lead by conveying vision. And as we've said, vision is useless if it cannot be conveyed inspirationally. So as we approach the hiring process, it is our job to get a feeling for a candidate's verbal acumen. Included in this is both the written and spoken word. How strong is their vocabulary? How well read are they? Do they speak in an engaging manner? How is their posture? Do they make eye contact?

[Ross Blaising]

As we write this, I am reminded of an anecdote that from a previous position that I had as a developer for a large organization in Atlanta. I worked under a Regional Partner who was very supportive my efforts. He was an exceptional advocate of his teams and would brag about us internally and externally. In closed-door discussions, he would tell me how impressed and confident he was with my team's work. Much of this derived from the fact that I could sit down with him and tell him everything that he needed to know in a way that he could hear it. It let him know that I understood what mattered most to him as well as to the projects. If I were talking to the CFO, I would convey the same information very differently. (As we've discussed, to inspire or to inspire confidence we need to be able to approach people from the place that inspires them, not us.) When, as the regional leader, he would compliment me or my team for our preparedness or presentations, I used to reply to him that 'I was just a salesman.' Invariably his face would invariably scrunch up like he had just bit into a lemon, clearly not liking that conclusion.

I would think to myself, of course I knew how to build a building. Of course I knew how to manage a project. Of course I knew how to hit dates and manage a team. All of this was expected. The ability that I had that was the great differentiator was that I could convey vision, certainty and excitement to those around me. This made them feel confident in their roles on the team and confident of my leadership. Consequently this allowed me the breathing room to do what I needed without much interference. I understood that my job was to 'sell' the product of my team, myself, and our portfolio to those below, adjacent to, and above me. So like I said, 'I'm just a salesman.'

Vocabulary. The first aspect that we want to understand is their vocabulary. After all, one cannot use words engagingly if they don't understand their meanings. Fortunately, a candidate's vocabulary has been tested and quantified and their results normed against their peers multiple times. We simply need to request their SAT, LSAT, GRE or GMAT score transcripts as part of their Application Package.

Writing. The second aspect of establishing the communicative aptitudes of the candidate comes from their ability to write convincingly. This is also addressed in the GMAT and LSAT scores, but more importantly in the essay section of our specific Application Package (to be discussed in chapter 12). The point of the essay is to be able to have each candidate pontificate on the same issue. That way we can evaluate their abilities to construct a cogent and compelling argument side by side. It is not necessarily important that their answer is correct (if there is even the possibility for a correct answer) or whether we even agree with their conclusions. The point is how they present their logic, progression and style.

Verbal. Lastly, we need a feel for their ability to function well in face-to-face situations. As developers, we are required to be compelling in front of a single person, small groups and sometimes large auditoriums. Our audiences range from eager to hostile. For a seasoned orator with a robust set of tools, each of these permutations are the same – or at least present equal opportunities. So when evaluating our candidates, we want to gain a molecular understanding of the candidate's ability and confidence in speaking in a range of situations.

It may seem like we are really placing a lot of emphasis on gaining an understanding of the candidate's conveyance skills. That is absolutely correct. While there are no guarantees as to any individual's success, we have to stay focused on our primary goal of the evaluation process; we are here to isolate and quantify the traits that will identify the candidates who have the statistically highest percentage chance of success in our programs. There is no other quality that predicts future success in a leadership role better than one's ability to convey concepts, facts or ideas clearly, concisely, compellingly. We really want to get this one right.

It is also our belief that people tend to be pretty consistent across these categories. In other words, if a candidate has an aptitude in one of the areas, they will likely have it in two or three. What we need to remember is that these future developers have also not had the time to hone their skills in the way that we have. We are trying to identify their potential, rather than their progress. If they happen to be very polished, then that is great.

Of the three conveyance skills (vocabulary, written and verbal), perhaps the most crucial from our perspective is vocabulary. This probably sounds a bit counterintuitive because really, does knowing all the words actually make one more successful? No, it does not. But at issue here are three things:

First, the bulk of our vocabulary is established in the first quarter of our lives, so if we don't have a strong one by the time that we are 20 or 25, then we will likely not ever have one. Vocabulary is the issue that we can 'do' the least about.

Second, people typically develop much of their vocabularies not through memorizing word lists but rather through voracious reading. Reading not only provides definition, but shows words in a context. Strong readers tend to use words more correctly and understand their appropriateness and nuance better than those do not read regularly or in quantity.

Third, the importance of a strong vocabulary is not to show people how smart we are or to impress them by conjuring obscure or complicated word usages. In fact, the job of a compelling speaker is quite the opposite: it is to adjust language, tone and cadence so that a message is deliverable to the audience in a way that they can understand it and make effective use of it. The importance of a strong vocabulary is that it allows us to understand our audience. The fact is that the other two aspects of verbal dexterity (written and spoken aptitudes) are more easily developable. They can be honed through our mentorship programs.

History of success. We've all heard the phrase 'The greatest predictor of future success is past performance.' Chances are that we all know the wisdom of that statement. Regardless of whether they are able to do so because of genetic predisposition or because something was learned through adolescent environments or it is just a product of sheer will, we want people who succeed. It is the authors' belief that the determinants of a 'history of success' are actually a combination of these. In *The Art of War*, Sun Tzu says, "Victorious warriors win first and then go to war, while defeated warriors go to war first and then seek to win." To paraphrase, 'Every battle is won or lost before it is ever fought.'

This effectively means that success and failure are choices that we make. Of course, saying that you are going to succeed does not mean that you will win, but people who choose to succeed behave differently than those who don't. The refusal to fail, if it is really internalized, precipitates action and preparedness and expertise. People who choose to succeed also make that choice in everything that they do.

We believe, along with Sun Tzu, that we are each individually predisposed to success or failure. And when you observe the people in your own life, it is hard to deny that there are some who always seem to succeed and some who always seem to fail, regardless of the tasks that are placed before them. We have all known people who, no matter how large or difficult the goal with which they are tasked, will be able meet and exceed those expectations.

Conversely, we have also known those for whom we could lower the bar to virtually any level and they would still miss it by fifteen percent. There are people to whom we could say, 'I don't care what you accomplish all day, just be to work by 9 a.m.' – and they would still regularly show up at 9:15 a.m. These are the broken individuals that we need to weed out.

What are the components of generally consistent success? We use the qualifier 'generally consistent' because there always exists the X-factor of luck, good or bad. And it would not be fair to assume that ultimate success or failure is always solely in the hands of any one person.

However, we do believe that individuals with a generally consistent history of success tend to score highly in one or both of two categories: natural talent and exceptional work ethics. Ideally our search will deliver candidates who score high in both, but that is often not the case. Of those who excel because they 'just get it,' often they have not developed the most rigorous work ethics because it just hasn't been necessary. At the same time, those that succeed through a work ethic often have another potent quality, a burning desire to win. They will not allow themselves to be beaten. It would be difficult to say if one of these paths to success is better than the other, as both result in the same destination.

[Ross Blaising]

In my younger years (through high school) I was always a competent student, but never really reached my potential. Truth be told, I was generally bored. I would read my lessons through once or take notes during class and didn't ever really study. I always knew that I could show up to most tests and perform to a B+/A- level without really trying. This was the result of a very naturally strong 'get-it factor.' The downside to that aptitude is that, in my youth, I never developed a strong work ethic. It was not until college, when I was competing with folks who were strong in both talent and effort, that I was forced to play a game of catch-up. It was then that I really gained an appreciation for hard work. In years since, as I talk with friends who perhaps did take those early studies more seriously, I do wonder how my path might have been different had I worked harder.

Our challenge during the evaluation process is to identify a predisposition for success. Undoubtedly, this is one of the most difficult qualities to 'absolutely quantify' during the interview process. Not only are we limited by the amount of time that we spend with each candidate, but they are also so early in their career paths that there have been few opportunities for individual professional success or for them to prove themselves. Exceptional circumstances aside, we will likely leave the interviews with, at best, a 'fuzzy' belief that they have this trait. In the end of course, we must trust our team's collective 'gut feel' on the subject.

Fortunately, success is typically verifiable and there are tools at our disposal, which we will discuss in chapter 12 on candidate selection:

1. *Honors and Awards.* It is not uncommon to request this information, as it is a part of most college application packages and resumes. When we do request this information, context would be useful. We suggest requiring the candidate include a paragraph explaining each honor or award.

2. *Essay.* Typical essay questions include those that require the candidate to describe situations of adversity in their lives. How did they deal with them? What did they learn from the situation? What they might do differently? It is not unreasonable to direct the essay question in a way that might have them tie their answer to an issue that led to a significant success.

3. *References.* Another opportunity that often goes underutilized in the hiring process deals with the checking of references. Typically, the process is either handled by a recruiter, HR representative or an assistant. The information gleaned tends to be along the lines of: How long have you known the candidate? In what capacity? Would you recommend them to work for me or my company? What is their greatest quality? What is their greatest deficiency?

Failing to really mine the data on a candidate can be a glaringly 'missed opportunity' for an organization to gain an understanding of the candidate. As such, we might suggest the following:

a. On the reference sheet of the Application Package, have the candidate provide a narrative context of their relationship with the reference, including its length and capacity.

b. Have the candidate describe which of their personal qualities the reference will best be able to address.

c. Before narrowing the candidate pool, have the references screened by a member of the evaluation team for all of the 'typical' information described above. Have them take copious notes. Then once the pool has been filtered to the final four to six candidates, assign a candidate to each member of the hiring team and have them call one of the references for a 15-30 minute interview to discuss the candidate in depth. Direct the interview to filling 'holes' in the Application Package.

d. Whenever possible leave the option open to have a follow-up discussion with the reference, to fill in any final holes in the candidate profile.

4. *Interviews.* During the interview portion of the process, have the candidate describe in detail aspects of their lives of which they are proudest, most disappointed, hoping to improve, etc. and how they played into their listed successes. We will say this over and over: Because we are making a six-plus year

commitment, we need to make sure we are getting the answers necessary to make the best decision possible.

One of the questions that typically arises when formulating the evaluation package and process is: 'Do the candidate's described successes need to be real estate development specific?' If we are admitting to our programs only young professionals who have recently completed their undergraduate or graduate educations or with only a few years' experience, then the answer would be have to be 'no.' We would already assume that they have little-to-no relevant real estate experience, and therefore it would be almost impossible for them to have had any real estate development success. At this point in their careers, the candidates' successes and failures are likely limited to scholastic endeavors, sports, clubs, etc.

Because our maxim is that success and failure are often consistent trends in individuals, we should not get too hung-up on the diversity of successes. Other than very specific examples (i.e., Rhodes Scholarship, etc.), it is difficult to assign a value to the achievements, and getting into ranking the 'quality' of the successes would be defocusing to the leadership committee.

If it is important to the team to rank the candidates' success traits (outside of the distinctions of natural talent and work ethic as described above), then timeline tends to be a more useful metric. For instance, candidates with more recent histories of success might score higher than those whose examples predominantly occurred earlier in life.

We could also evaluate the competitive nature of the success. For instance, someone who achieved the status of Eagle Scout (due to the rigorous dedication and difficulty associated with that honor) might rank higher than an award-winning drummer from a band, etc. It is very subjective. Even so, our goal is to establish a consistent pattern of success in an individual and to understand whether that pattern is more likely the results of natural talent or hard work or both, not to validate our opinions of their individual successes.

Get It Factor. The 'Get It Factor' (GIF) is closely related to the I.Q., as we discussed above in our toolbox section, in that it too is a cognitive ability. Where it is different than an overall I.Q. is that we are looking at specific aspects of the tool. For our purposes, the aspects of intelligence that we are referring to with the 'get it factor' are reasoning and the ability to perceive relationships between things. The GIF is one's ability to take disparate pieces of data and assemble them into patterns, then into information, and then draw conclusions from that information, which are then turned into action. Similar to I.Q., the critical factor is speed. Remember the Stephen Hawking example.

Having just discussed the History of Success (HOS) as the second most important soft-skill with which to evaluate a candidate, it might seem that both the HOS and the GIF would be intrinsically linked. However, oddly enough, they may be wholly unrelated. Consistent success often derives from one of two avenues: hard work or talent. The GIF is essentially the natural talent found with those who have a strong history of success. So if we say above that both natural talent and work ethic can get us to the same result, why then would natural talent (GIF) have its own category in third place on the soft-tools list?

On a basic level, the difference in a project's end result may be miniscule between someone who succeeds due to natural talent rather than methodical dedication. There are however areas that are specific to real estate development success in which natural talent is superior to a strong work ethic. For instance, someone with a high GIF will likely distinguish themselves in settings such as public speaking, which is critical to our success as developers. People with the combination of high GIFs and verbal acumen are often considered to be clever or witty (which most people associate with intelligent), or have higher probabilities of being charismatic, etc. Therefore, we can expect that people endowed with both the first soft-tool and the third will also be strong in the second. If they are somehow not, then we will likely find that they lack the will to succeed.

To drive the point even further, often the riskiest and therefore most critical point in a project is at its inception, when the developer is describing his vision to a community (neighborhood, abutters, etc.), the local commissioners and planning and zoning officials, in hopes of winning their trust, and ultimately entitlements. Verbal slip-ups or gaffes at this stage can be the death knell for the developer's plans.

It is at this point that the developer must be able to think on his feet. It is while faced with this adversity that he must be his most compelling and inspirational. Where a Get It Factor helps most is for the developer's ability to address the often varied and sometimes illogical whims of the audience. In this case, simple and rigorous preparation can be less important than a strong Get It Factor and charisma.

Secondary Soft-tools. For as much as the 'primary' soft-tools described above are important for real estate developers, they are also key success factors for almost any leadership role of consequence, regardless of industry. If candidates who score highly in those three categories are properly identified in the admissions process, our program's chance of success will be drastically higher (from a talent perspective at least). Of course we still need to develop and implement a curriculum that makes use of our associates' potential and builds skills in a logical order.

As we have said so many times, our individual organizations are unique to our set of values and corporate vision. Therefore, our proposed set of primary soft-tools is not an exhaustive list. Each organization will likely have additional 'secondary' qualities that must be added, per the leadership team, which will help to tailor and fine-tune the evaluation process to our unique needs. Some tools that may help to round out our final lists may also include the following (as well as others):

Hunger. Anyone who has been in real estate development for any length of time understands how susceptible our business models are to the various market oscillations, expansions and contractions. Due to the relative illiquidity of our product and lengthy project lifecycles, we experience even slight changes very vividly. Undoubtedly, when conditions are good for developers they are very good; and conversely when they are bad, they can be very bad. Even when we are in a positive growth cycle, important projects can be lost or delayed due to building moratoriums, unreasonable or reactionary communities, unforeseen soil and ecological conditions, etc. Sometimes it is only our 'unending spring of self-confidence' that keeps us moving forward.

So whether we call it hunger, or drive, or passion for real estate development, it is this love of the rewards and responsibilities of our profession that can pull us from the depths of frustration and doubt that will invariably and repeatedly occur throughout our careers. Like any prizefighters, we are going to take our share of punches and we are going to get knocked down. And while the 'primary' soft-tools will help us to fight smarter and anticipate and avoid some of the more devastating blows, our hunger will help to deliver the stamina to stay in the ring for one more round.

Values. A significant portion of chapter 3 discussed the importance of being a values-based organization. Our corporate values operate as a backbone and galvanizing force for the culture of our firms. They reflect the beliefs that we hold important for our profession. At the same time they are informed by our personal values. Values give us the compass with which we navigate the complexities of the world. By now, we have all probably figured out that when we operated counter to our values, we may profit in the short-term, but we do thrive and prosper. We cannot be our best selves while rejecting our values. This behavior never leads to happiness.

Then in chapter 4, we discussed the importance of marketing these values. We spoke of telling our candidates what our values are, so that we do not waste their time and they do not waste ours. These should apply to real estate and non-real estate values alike. Over the six-year mentorship program, we are going to get to know our associates intimately, and while we would never expect that our associates have our exact set of beliefs and goals (after all, they are very young), we really do want to know what they were taught to value in this world. Values alignment goes directly to their long-term fit. As such, our candidates' beliefs and goals cannot be ignored in the admissions process.

Appearance. It can be argued whether appearance is a hard or a soft skill. And in truth it is both; it is a discipline as well as a propensity. The initial question to be answered is whether the candidate, if properly taught how to present themselves, would be able to do it. The ultimate goal is to understand whether or not the candidate takes pride in their appearance. For instance, are their clothes neatly pressed and reasonably well matched, is their hair cut, are their nails appropriately manicured, are they overweight or do they appear slovenly? While none of these qualities necessarily have anything to do with their intelligence or capacity to learn what our programs intend to teach, it certainly does affect how well they will be able to implement what they have been taught.

One day the candidates that we train will be the embodiment of our organizations. They will represent our company, our beliefs and values in everything that they do, both at work and at play. Once admitted to our development schools, helping them to hone their look, get into shape (physical fitness may be a component of our programs) and develop a level of sartorial excellence, and so on will be part of our task. For now, do they appear to treat their bodies with the sense of respect that our organizations require? We are here to create the rockstars of the industry.

Conclusion. As we have repeated so many times, each admission to our program is a long-term strategic investment. When we learn about each candidate who hopes to come and learn from us, it matters much less where they have been, and much more about whether they have abilities and drive to complete our six-year journey. And while none of us has that clear of a crystal ball, our job remains to make the best, safest decisions for our unique organizations.

To achieve this, first we must clearly understand what it is that we value as a company. Second, we must know very honestly what skills are best suited for excellence in our industry. We need to know what our idea of the 'ideal' candidate looks like. Third, we need to methodically test and mine for those qualities that we value. And then feel confident that we are making the best, most informed decisions possible.

The authors recognize that hiring (or admissions) under our system is more laborious than at a 'typical' real estate development firm. That said, the preparation that we stress will allow us to gather much more targeted data efficiently and within a compact time frame.

Chapter 12

Old School, New School

"Winning isn't everything – but wanting to win is." – Vince Lombardi

Each of our past three chapters has focused on aspects of our Schools for Development as they relate to our new employees, focusing on these topics:

1. How do we shift our focus 'from us to them' so that we can properly mentor and grow them?
2. How do we use our marketing tools to reach them?
3. What qualities should we look for in our future hires?

What is clear from the combination of these is that we believe the first step to our success is building a company upon the right people. Our next question is 'how do we best evaluate them as a fit for our program?' Equally obvious, and perhaps seemingly daunting, is that rooting out all of the information that we want to know in making our hiring decisions is terrifically laborious. There is just so much to consider.

TSORE simplifies this morass by breaking it down into easily digestible, bite-sized chucks, so that they can be addressed individually. Our (the authors' and the readers') expertise as senior developers and owners of our firms, along with our previously thought out knowledge of what we seek in a student, combined with logical systemization will remove much of the potential chaos from the hiring process. The efficiency of the process will allow us time to inject targeted moments of creativity into the process without losing focus.

Even though not a syllable has yet been written to describe what the actual process of admissions for your School for Development should resemble, if we remain true to form, you can probably surmise that something revolutionary is about to emerge. The answer is both yes and no. Yes, in that we are about to suggest a model that no real estate development firm has likely ever employed. And no, in that the model does exist, just not within our industry. So we are not reinventing the wheel here. Instead, we are removing an old set of bent rims with worn down tires, and replacing them with a set of balanced and precision-machined wheels clad with steel-belted Michelin tires. In other words, the ride is about to get a lot safer and smoother.

The current system. As the process unfolds through the following pages, keep in mind the contrast between the current 'typical' system of hiring, which relies on acquiring experienced or semi-experienced young developers with a set of hard-skills, which we did not teach, who are furnished to us by recruiters who we compensate at $20K+ per hire. The result is that once we have hired the new team member, we can expect to keep them for 2-4 years, until either (a) our organization is no longer teaching them the skills that they want, or (b) we are no longer paying them the highest salary in the market. At that point they become a free agent. Once they leave our firm a call is again placed to that same recruiter, where we ask them to steal another young developer from one of our competitors.

So our value proposition for enticing our next hire to jump to our team is that we will pay them a salary at the current top of the market, and the cycle begins again. In the end, we choose to pay considerable acquisition fees and the highest salary possible to get talent trained at firms that we feel we are inferior to ours, and whom we expect to retain for no more than one or two project cycles. This strategy feels absurd.

A new approach. Rather than continuing the cycle of this 'dog endlessly chasing his own tail,' TSORE firms find young, inexperienced candidates with very different skills and aptitudes, and through the promise of mentorship and a seven-year education, grow and retain our talent without paying periodic consulting fees to our recruiting industry friends. This system increases our talent retention and decreases our unnecessary employee acquisition costs. Big picture, we shift the chaos of human capital churn from the marketplace to within our firm's control. The value of that stability is huge.

Admissions

As we stated above, the system for efficiently evaluating large quantities of disparate data on multiple applicants is not unknown to the world, just to our industry. Considering that we have been calling our firms 'Schools for Development' for over 100 pages now, it shouldn't be too surprising that the model to follow is best observed in our universities. After all, the higher education industry is tasked with weeding through thousands and sometimes tens of thousands of prospective applicants annually in order to select the relatively few who will be the best fit for their institutions. While our firms will only be tasked with weeding through a couple dozen candidates, we can repurpose some important portions of their very sophisticated machine to help us efficiently reach our end goals.

How do we evaluate them? Because we begin with the maxim that we are looking for relatively inexperienced candidates armed with raw talent and dreams of one day being like us, we shouldn't shy away from the premise that our applicants really know little to nothing that will be practically useful in the profession. They are mostly-blank slates of talent and potential –exactly as we want them to be. Our job during the admissions process is to identify and evaluate that potential as it relates to the long-term needs and goals for their success. Therefore, the industry standard of simply collecting and evaluating resumes is pointless. In fact, let's just agree to throw the resume out; cast it aside. It will do nothing but mislead us. This is important for a few reasons:

1. First, how much can we really glean from a resume that describes zero to two years of real world experience?
2. Second, most resumes are designed to convey hard-skills that we have already agreed are unimportant to our decision process.
3. Third, resumes convey what the candidate wants us to know about them, described in the light in which they want it shown. Reviewing resumes makes us a passive part of the initial evaluation process. With a resume that they created, we abdicate our leadership in the evaluation process.

So now that we are unshackled from the spurious security of a file full of resumes in one of our cabinet drawers, we must embrace a different candidate evaluation strategy. And it begins with a few simple premises:

Formalize the Process. We should never underestimate the value that our organization is very unique. The criteria we use to evaluate the applicants are also unique. After all, consider the time and effort that has taken place by creating, honing and enveloping our vision and values into the DNA of this new firm.

With this exclusiveness our new business model and marketing has the opportunity of being much more appealing to individuals with the potential of becoming sophisticated developers. We should therefore expect a larger number of higher qualified applicants. Accordingly, we need to have a very structured and standardized process and evaluation package that gleans the information that is important to us and allows us to easily compare one candidate to the next.

As we have articulated, the information that we will base our ultimate decisions on is harder to ascertain than simply 'I worked here. I did this. I learned that...' So to accomplish our goal of isolating and admitting only candidates with the most extensive 'toolboxes,' we recommend developing a uniquely tailored, comprehensive application package (similar to a university application).

Hire only once or twice per year. Part of the value proposition of our development university is that we have tailored a multi-year path for the education of our students. What we have learned over the past chapters is that the program suggested in this book is more time and energy intensive than more typical models. Of course we believe that in the big picture, the benefits of a more stabilized workforce and well-trained developers will easily outweigh the initial time outlays. Upfront planning will decrease considerably the potential chaos and will pay dividends in both efficiency and treasure. And one of the most important areas to regulate is when hiring occurs.

Think of it this way, if you apply to a university, your education begins and ends at specific intervals (semesters). For a university to abandon that system would result in chaos, inefficiency and ultimately, failure. Now within your firm, imagine hiring three first-year associates (the first in February, the second in June and the third in September) and trying to cohesively train them. During each of their six years in the program, each candidate would be at a different place in their education and we would be required to teach each and every lesson three times, as opposed to one. That sort of inefficiency quickly becomes unmanageable and eventually our systems would break down.

From an interviewing perspective, there is also a tremendous advantage to having singular, defined dates to the process. Of course, planning the process out on our annual calendars means that we reduce our last minute shuffling and the difficulties of getting the entire admissions committee onto the same page. Also, consider the advantage to the prospective student, who can now go to your website and clearly see the list of items that they will need to assemble, as well as all submission dates, interview dates, etc. Simple planning and posting can make this fairly complicated process painless and even fun.

Compete for the job. Many years ago, when we applied to college, we were given the choice to apply to institutions that were highly selective, moderately selective, or not selective at all. There were and are educational products for all goals, income brackets and aptitudes. By choosing to operate our companies with the TSORE principles, we are opting to be a highly selective organization. As such, we can expect that candidates who are attracted to our organization have already bought in to our concept, are prepared to dedicate their training and future to us, and believe that they are more deserving of this opportunity than their competitors. And they will welcome the opportunity to prove it. The question then is 'How?'

Phase 1. Data Collection

Step 1. The first thing that we need to do is to advertise the values of our firm. The most obvious application of this is in our web presence. We have already expounded on this subject in chapter 9. For as much as we are invigorated by the vision and morals of the firms we create, we must also remember that they are not for everyone. But those who do embrace them will do so vigorously. In addition to your website clearly articulating 'who you are' and what you stand for,' you must also illuminate the path for the prospective developer to become your student.

Most corporate websites have a careers section that lists various job opportunities or a link to submit a resume. Using similar nomenclature on your website is fine. Once inside the 'careers' section however, it is important to remember that the process that we discuss in *The Soul of Real Estate* is only for the development team. Depending upon the anatomy of your specific firm, there may disciplines in addition to development, such as property management, construction, acquisitions, finance, etc. Remember not to comingle your messaging. Keep the development group discrete.

Once in the development section of the website, be explicit. Tell them exactly why they should apply to your program. As we recall, it is not a terrifically more complex version of: "The value proposition that my organization offers is that in seven years, you will be a developer. Because of my structure and program, in half a decade you will be my partner, or you can leave me and be qualified to be a partner at any company in the country. Mine is a school for development."

We need to explain:

- Our unique methodology
- Career development timeline
- Hiring process (submission timeline, a link to the admissions package)

By being explicit, we make both their choice as whether to apply and the application process easy on them – and on us at the same time.

One concern that we may have in placing all of this information out there is 'Isn't this all proprietary? If I put my secret formula out there, can't someone just copy it?' The answer is simply 'No.' As we go through the process of designing our firm, it will be very clear that the time and thought processes that result in our ultimate business model are very specific to each of us. We are much more than a collection of stock photos and lofty verbiage. Firm who adopt the rhetoric without the intensive foundation work that we discuss will not be able to deliver on their promise and will be exposed as frauds.

Plus, the 'secret sauce' is in this book. A thousand new firms may be created from reading TSORE, and each will be its own unique snowflake. What we provide is a methodology and guidance for structuring firms of the future; however, each iteration is unique to the values and vision of your leadership.

Step 2. Suggest that they read Part I of *The Soul of Real Estate* before they ever apply. Although it may appear somewhat self-serving, there is more 'context' described in those hundred pages than can easily be conveyed on a website or brochure. Even though we will each take and adapt the concepts in this book to our individual organizations, it does provide a seminal thread of principles that will help to inform our applicants of what to expect within the program for which they are applying. We want candidates that are completely dedicated to the education that we will provide, and the more informed they are before they apply, the easier time we will all have.

Step 3. Discussed above, the process of receiving and evaluating resumes is a passive form of recruitment. And under the TSORE rubric, it is unlikely that they convey any information that will be relevant to your hiring decision anyway. This of course does not mean that we propose no longer collecting data that might be found on a resume; rather that each firm asks for only the very specific information that they want and that it is input in a singular format. What this allows the managers to do is to look at consistent information side by side in the same format, thereby making comparisons easier and increasing the efficiency of the comparison. The application package thus provides us the opportunity to ask for the information that will assist us in narrowing the field of applicants. It also returns us to being the active force in the evaluation and hiring process.

Another advantage to publishing the contents and requirements of the application package is that it gives the breadth of information requested and marries it to a timeline. In addition to items such as work and educational history, there are multiple items that will help ascertain the candidate's values and toolbox. These may include:

- College transcripts and standardized test scores
- IQ and personality tests
- Supplemental questionnaires and essays
- Biographical and experiential data
- Video essays
- Reference requests

While the goal is not to be onerous in the data that is being collected, most of the data collection above is free to the development firm. The IQ test (which may be omitted in lieu of a SAT, GMAT, GRE or LSAT) and the personality test (Myers Briggs or other) are the only ones that incur cost. Although these tests are traditionally given once a candidate passes the initial hurdles of the interview process, we suggest collecting all data before ever commencing. The cost of these is minimal in comparison to the efficiency that is delivered to the organization.

At the conclusion of the Data Collection phase (which is technically the start of the weeding-out activities), the initial list of candidates is put through the sieve and candidates who did not complete the process correctly or are unqualified are removed from the prospective student pool. A 'thank you' letter is generated and the remaining candidates move to Phase 2.

Phase II. Vetting

Step 4. Now that the candidate pool has been reduced to a manageable number, a deeper understanding of our remaining prospective developers is in order. Among other more pedantic things, the data collection and analysis of the steps in Phase I were intended to develop a picture of the candidate's intelligence and Get It Factor. As we recall from chapter 9, these are two of the key components of the toolbox. Our current step, Phase II, is intended to achieve two goals;

1. Further solidify the beliefs about the candidate that were formed through data collection.

2. Ascertain the candidate's predisposition toward success.

While not a revolutionary step, we would like to reposition the 'check references' portion of the interview process to occur before ever meeting the prospect. In most traditional processes, checking the references occurs at the very end of the process, and is addressed as almost a formality. This course of action ignores an important investigative tool. Think of how many times we've heard, 'Well, all I need to do now is check your references and I think we have a deal.' This tells us two things: (1) The person hiring makes very important decisions more on 'gut' than data (which is risky), and (2) they don't respect the experiences and opinions of others. Neither of these should give us much confidence in their decision making process. What about when they are investing millions of investor dollars? What happens when their gut is wrong?

The inherent flaw in checking references at the end is that it places the conversation with the reference into the position of confirming or negating our beliefs about the candidate. Similar to our position on accepting resumes, back-loading the reference conversation distances us from our active role in ferreting-out the exact right candidate(s). A proactive, early conversation with the reference does two things:

1. Add richness to the eventual interviews with the candidate.
2. Provide another opportunity to reduce the number of the candidate pool (if they are not suitable).

So when it comes to scheduling the conversation with the references, there are of course some ways to make the experience more fruitful:

1. Do not hesitate to request reference information from the candidate on anyone who piques your interest in the data collection phase, regardless of whether they are on the candidate's reference list. If you think they may add insights, ask the candidate for their contact info.

2. Approach it as an interview. Ask the reference versions of the same questions that you will be asking the actual candidate.

3. Be prepared with active-voice questions. Avoid open-ended questions like 'Tell me about your experiences with ----?' or 'What is -----'s greatest weakness or strength?'

4. We have all heard throughout our lives that we learn much more from our mistakes than our failures. A candid conversation with someone both seasoned and intimate with those failures should tell us more about the candidate than their listing of their successes.

5. The reference check is a multi-step process. Be sure to let them know that you may need to speak with them again in the future.

Remember that the purpose of the entire interview process is to isolate the 'toolbox' of the candidate, so have a game plan and stick to it.

It is likely that calling three or four references for four candidates will be unduly cumbersome for one individual. Accordingly, you will likely want to divide the conversations up among each of the members of your admissions team. Rather than having each member of that team 'own' the conversations of a single candidate, consider distributing the reference checks for each potential student among each of the members, so that each one gets a flavor of each candidate. This strategy also lends itself to richer debate. Upon completion of the reference checks, make sure to distribute notes to each member of the admissions team.

Phase III. Interviews

It is finally time to meet the candidates. The research is done, information is compiled and conversations have been had. As always, because each firm is unique, the interview process will also be unique, not only firm by firm, but also year by year. And even though there is quite a bit of latitude with how this interview day is arranged, there are some specific components that should always and absolutely be present. While not an exhaustive list, the 'must have' components include:

1. *Individual interview with each member of the leadership team.* There is nothing new here. To increase the amount of information obtained, we suggest that each member of the admissions team be given the task of delving into a specific area of the applicants' potential and also that they take copious notes. To make the interviewers' job easier, the evaluators' package should include a list of questions to be asked at each interview as well as a section for general notes and even an area to rate their professionalism, posture, tone and

temperament, etc. As we have said so many times, organization helps everyone involved.

2. *Panel interview.* A great, high(er) pressure tool is the panel interview. Often more general in topics than the individual interview, panel style interviews give the team the ability to ask non-linear questions. It is also a great opportunity to observe a candidate field multiple-sourced questions. Some tools to really observe the candidate's composure are to increase and decrease cadence, and to ask both general and pointed questions.

3. *Additional essay.* Unlike the essay(s) that are submitted with the initial application package, a short, timed essay on a subject that is unrelated to development or the job for which they are applying gives the evaluator the ability to see how well the applicant can shift gears, think on their feet and form cohesive arguments.

Phase IV. Concluding the Process

The application, interview and acceptance process is intense for all parties. Once a final decision has been made it is important to recognize that everyone involved has run a serious gauntlet. In order to announce the accepted candidate and to show the proper respect for all who have competed in the process, rather than notifying the candidates by phone or email, we suggest that all final round participants be invited back to the office for the results.

Present the offer to the successful candidate(s) in person and before the group meeting. Negotiate their acceptance on the spot.

Considering the information that they had prior to their application, as well as the rigors that they have undergone during the process, there really should be no outstanding questions. This is an opportunity for them to reaffirm their commitment. After all, we are offering something that no one else in the market offers.

If there is any hesitation on the part of the applicant, we might consider doing everyone a favor and rescind the offer. That way we can go immediately to the next viable candidate and award them acceptance (provided that there were multiple qualified candidates). For obvious reasons we suggest not notifying the other candidates that they were not accepted until we have locked down the awardee(s).

Once we have committed ourselves to our new associate, there will be a few very disappointed applicants in a nearby room. Because we appreciate the time and efforts of those who made it to the final round and we may want them to reapply in the future, we should announce to each one privately that they did not make the final cut.

A phone or email rejection would not be terribly helpful to them as a final contact. Instead, invite each competitor to a non-mandatory final group exit interview. This is an opportunity for them to learn from the process and review the comments of the evaluators in the form of an exit package (which is another reason why we want to have a standardized evaluation form internally – it can provide a very useful take-away packet for the candidate). The group exit interview does not require a panel format or more than a half-hour of time. It is just a way to give helpful feedback and tips to those who want it.

As we've said before, our processes and focuses going forward are outwardly focused. The good will and reputation that having a well-run interview process and conscientious exit process will garner for us will greatly outweigh the small amount of additional time required. Imagine how each one of us would have appreciated a process like this in our early careers.

Other Issues.

Older Candidates. We briefly mentioned this earlier, but a situation that will undoubtedly arise is that there will be an applicant that has multiple years' experience in real estate development, and is not necessarily at the beginning of their career. What do we do with these candidates? On the one hand, they may know certain things that will make their education easier. On the other hand, a number of potential problems may arise:

1. What they have been taught might be incompatible with the values of our program and we are tasked with reprogramming and re-teaching them. As we stated, this ultimately adds time to our already intense program as well as potentially introducing unnecessary chaos to our efforts.

2. Rather than creating an atmosphere of camaraderie amongst the associates that is useful, the experienced associate may attempt to use their previous experience to establish themselves as a superior, which can disrupt the culture.

3. They may expect that their experience will allow them to 'test in' to an advanced year or pay grade.

Testing In. There is not an easy answer as to where we cut-off acceptance into the program. Each individual is unique and it is our job to evaluate the risks and make the best decision for our organization. And while we recognize that the ultimate choice will vary for organization to organization, we strongly suggest that we never allow an Associate to pass over (or test-in to) any advanced part of the education. For example, a candidate with four years' experience, who was previously making $90K may not be content entering our program as a first year associate making $50K. Remember, the key to the system is organization and consistency.

So now we have a new firm, a new attitude, a new website and a new employee...now what do we do?

Chapter 13

Onboarding

"Early impressions are hard to eradicate from the mind. When once wool has been dyed purple, who can restore it to its previous whiteness?" – Saint Jerome

Most of us can probably remember our first day of work. The elation of knowing that we were chosen from a given set of candidates was followed by a sense of pride in knowing that we had done well, which was then followed by the excitement that we were finally about to embark on our professional path. The euphoria lasted up until the evening before our first day of work, when nervousness began to set in. We didn't sleep well that night. We woke up early, got ready quickly and arrived at the office thirty minutes early. And then we waited.

The funny thing is that while for us this was an exciting beginning to a lifelong journey, to everyone else at the office, it was just Monday. So when our handler arrived on time, they showed us around the office and where we would sit. We were introduced to so many people that we couldn't remember any of their names, and then we met with HR and IT. The entire experience was overwhelming in the most underwhelming way possible.

But it shouldn't be this way. And more importantly, it doesn't have to be.

'Onboarding' is a term that most of us are probably not too familiar with. It is a discipline that was not in formal existence when

228

we matriculated. And with the exception of some very large companies, onboarding is a series of activities that have historically been neither formalized nor held in high regard. As to what onboarding actually is there are multiple definitions, but Wikipedia defines it as follows: "Onboarding, also known as organizational socialization, refers to the mechanism through which new employees acquire the necessary knowledge, skills, and behaviors to become effective organizational members and insiders." And while that definition sounds both comprehensive and official, for our purposes, it is much simpler:

"Onboarding is how we get our new Associate integrated into our team physically, mentally and culturally."

As with our discussions on leadership, integrity and salesmanship, the subject of onboarding is becoming a much wider field of study, and consequently, its own industry. There are hundreds of articles and books on the subject. Rather than get into the minutia of exactly how onboarding best occurs, our goal is to hit a few of the high points that can make our new employee integration much more memorable and fruitful for all parties.

First and foremost, be prepared. *If* we have spent days narrowing down our candidate pool, and a few more days interviewing them and deciding who to hire. *If* we have prepared and submitted an offer letter. *If* we have agreed to the date upon which their education begins. If we have done all of those things, then we really have no excuse to be unprepared for their arrival. So we should have a plan.

And not just a plan for their first couple of weeks. Fully integrating a new Associate is a process that will take about 90 days.

By thinking out the strategy and goals of those most important three months, we can better monitor the Associates' assimilation into the group. We can stem bad behaviors and potential conflicts before they have time to grow or fester. And during this period where their canvases are most pristine, we can ensure that they fully embrace our vision and culture. A culturally 'bought-in' employee is a most effective employee.

Our approach to the 90-day onboarding process breaks down into two primary phases that are designed to serve the same goal of indoctrination, but have differing intensity levels. We entitle these:

Phase I. The first seven days

Phase II. Days eight through ninety

While these are not terrifically clever monikers, they do bring to bear a certain subtle level of clarity. In the first phase, we are trying to capture and maintain the inherent excitement that new Associate arrives with on their first day on the job. We also want to leverage their openness into trust. The second phase continues to build upon the established trust, albeit at a reasoned pace. During days eight through ninety, we fold in additional tools and support to allow them to more quickly become stable and productive members of the team.

PHASE I. The First Seven Days

Make the first week count. The opportunity to leverage those high emotions and excitement that we describe in the first few paragraphs of this chapter dissipates quickly. All of that initial hope and wonderment provides us with a natural advantage, which we may exploit into further trust and openness. Trust translates into cultural buy-in and a willingness to learn.

Of course we are introducing the new Associates into our systems and technology. They are getting to know their team and seeing a development pipeline for the first time. These are all the things that would happen at any firm. Where we differ slightly is that we want to make them feel special. When we hired them, they won a huge prize. It was a competition and they were the victors. So we give them some spoils. Here's what we do:

The gift bag. When the new Associate is shown their desk for the first time, there should be a swag bag waiting for them. Have it filled with items that incorporate them into the group. A signed welcome card. Have their business cards printed and ready before they arrive (they will immediately feel official). Include their personal coffee mug with either the company logo or their name on it. A $25 Starbucks gift card is a fine touch. Perhaps include a nice pen. Have their laptop already situated at their desk. Simple items will make them feel immediately welcome. And it does not have to be expensive.

Take them to lunch. Have at least one of the partners take them out to a great lunch. Eat fillet or lobster. Drink bourbon with them in the afternoon. Make it over the top. Sell them on the great future of this organization. Tell them how it came to be. Let them hear the firm's story from the man / men who started it all. Maybe take them to the shooting range after lunch and blow off a couple clips from an

AR15. The key is to sell them on the big picture and that they are now a part of something special. Let them know that one day, their story will be part of a legend.

Meet and greet. Throw a welcoming party. Most firms have a set of vendors that they work with regularly. Whether these are architects, attorneys, designers, contractors, local banking contacts, engineers or others, invite them all to meet your new developer. Of course this is also an opportunity for the firm to host an open house or drinks at a local watering hole. We know that these events do natural wonders for the internal and external teams as a whole; all we are suggesting is that we have the theme: 'Come and celebrate our new talent.'

The party does not have to be a swanky affair to achieve its goal, but it does need to be in the Associate's honor. One thing to keep in mind is that our young employee is still in their early to mid-twenties and they may not be accustomed to a lot of attention from older professionals. The party may be a little intimidating or overwhelming. So have a couple of other Associates or support staff assigned to make sure that our guests of honor are meeting people and not getting bogged down in too many long conversations. This event will go a long way toward maintaining that positive momentum as well as making it that much easier when they pick up the phone to call that architect or whomever.

Assign a peer coach. We spent a lot of time in Part I discussing the value of mentorship in our School for Development. Much of our context revolved around how we, as leaders, could embrace mentorship as a primary focus of the firm. The truth is that the culture of the firm flows from us. And so if we are committed mentors, then the culture become one of mentorship, and that makes everyone a mentor.

One of the responsibilities of more senior Associates (perhaps 4th year and above) is to become a peer mentor to our younger Associates. This allows them to assist in the onboarding process, alleviate us from handling the more mundane aspects of tutelage, and most important, perpetuates the value of mentorship to our future partner. And should that senior Associate move on to another firm or start their own once they have completed our program, then we have pollinated another organization with our values, further spreading our influence within the development world.

There are a multitude of permutations as to how that first week of our new Associate's employment may look. But by adding the three simple steps: an executive lunch, a welcome party and the assignment of a peer counselor, we have the opportunity to make that experience considerably more special. Each of the components are designed to reiterate to them that they are winners, that we value them, and that we want them to have the tools and support to succeed. Every firm may have additional components that they also want to incorporate, and as we choose exactly what activities we would like to incorporate into that first five days, the key is to apply our outward focused 'it's not about us, it's about them' philosophy. Our goal in this week is for a few big moments that will be most impactful.

PHASE II. Days Eight Through Ninety

Having completed the first week of their employment, all of our lives are getting back to normal and we are again, fully focused on the business of buying, selling and building. We will still be very hands-on with our first year Associates because, after all, they only have one weeks' experience. But our focus does shift from celebrating them to training them. That said, there are some tools that we can deliver that will make their steep learning curve feel less daunting.

Post-meeting meetings. First and foremost, do not make the mistake of treating your new Associates like a traditional Development Associate from those traditional firms who get locked in a closet to run proformas, reforecasts and assist with monthly owner's reports. We have to let them see the sun sometimes if we expect them to grow. So take them to at least one or two meetings per week.

There is a tremendous value to sitting in an OAC meeting and listening to the various stakeholders debate items that are germane to the project. It is also an opportunity for them to observe your leadership. The fact is that for the first year or so, the Associate will be inundated with industry-specific words and concerns that mean nothing to them. But they need to hear these words and learn our language sooner than later.

One of the best ways to further trust with our young hires is to help them make the world make sense. When they attend meetings with you, initially have their primary job at these meetings be to make notes of everything they didn't understand. After each meeting, commit to a short, fifteen minute after-meeting with the Associate where they can ask all of the things from their list. Explain the concepts so that they can understand them and watch their knowledge and competence grow.

Let them make low-level decisions. Our goal in training our Associates for six years is that we want them to be able to consistently make high-quality decisions. We do this so that we can trust that their decisions are sound and that we do not need to micro-manage them. We also do this so that we can leave the office and have a life with our families without the constant fear that we cannot trust in our firms' security when we are not there. To that end, we are going to teach them everything we can on the myriad of subjects that we consider when we make decisions. These range from art of design, to construction techniques, legal and financing structures, leadership techniques and even moral dilemmas. We need them to weigh it all when they make choices, just like we do.

But separate from the importance of making sound critical decisions, there is also the importance of just making decisions. So from the very beginning, we must provide the opportunity for our Associates to weigh alternatives and make a choice. Of course, in those earlier months and even years, we will monitor the decisions that they make. As we do this, our job is to evaluate the decisions themselves and also the methodologies employed in reaching them. When the outcomes are not catastrophic, we must let their decisions play out. We must also discuss the consequences of those decisions with the Associate and consistently challenge them to think broadly.

Weekly lunch with their peer mentor. In the first phase of onboarding, the new Associate was assigned a senior Associate as their handler. The job of this person is to mentor and aid them as they have questions throughout their first months in the firm. Because much of the initial work in assimilating the new Associate is not really partner-level work, a peer should be able to handle 90% of the day-to-day questions and advice giving.

In addition to the normal questions and concerns that an Associate will have about office operations, there will undoubtedly be concerns about office personalities, power structures, and the effectiveness of the School of Development, as well as the positioning of the firm within the market. Rather than pretend that these will not occur, create a safe space for it to happen. Create a space that is outside of the confines of the office. The offsite lunch is that space. Unlike the post-meeting meeting, which is topically very directed to the meeting that immediately preceded it, the peer mentor is there to help with these more global issues. No subjects are off the table. And of course, spending time away from the office with a mentor helps to foster trust and camaraderie.

Book club. The amount of inputs and considerations necessary to successfully navigate the development world is well outside the ability to be housed in any one given firm. Even if the firm contains expertise in capital, architectural or interior design, capital structures, urban design, construction techniques and legal acumen, it is impossible that those resources are exhaustive. Otherwise, we would not utilize consultants. But even if we could afford to house all of those professions comprehensively under a single roof, it would be terribly inefficient to utilize them primarily in the training of others.

Fortunately, almost every single input upon which the developer relies has an entire industry built around engaging debate on and furthering their theoretical and pragmatic discourse. It is in our best interest to utilize the work of others, whether that is from a book, movie, workshop or blog. We needn't reinvent the wheel. But we only help ourselves by systematizing the way in which these outside influences and ideas enter our organization. One great way to do that is to have a book club or podcast club.

In order for the book club to succeed however, we, the thought and culture leaders of the firm, must be its active propagators and participants. It cannot simply be a reading assignment for the Associate. So we must recognize, when we initiate a book club, that it is a commitment for all involved. It is also one of those items which becomes a part of the culture and will likely not end at the completion of onboarding.

As with our discussion of Phase I, the second phase of the onboarding contains four items that are important, but not comprehensive. Depending on each firm's focus, location, history and values, these items will be personalized and augmented appropriately. And while it may sound like a lot of work, it will be easier than we think. Especially considering that these items become part of our DNA. The extra things that we choose to do in our firm very quickly become simply the things we do.

Chapter 14

Archetype I – The Leader

"The reasonable man adapts to the world around him.
The unreasonable man expects the world to adapt to him.
Therefore, all progress is made by unreasonable men."
– H.D. Thoreau

On multiple occasions throughout Part I of *The Soul of Real Estate*, we have described our young developers as Masters of the Universe, and we have called them young CEOs, Leaders or Salesmen. We have tossed out these monikers and defended their use as being components necessary for the leaders of the profession. And we are only concerned with creating the leaders of our profession. Let our competitors train the lackeys.

Considering the amount of time spent trying to identify the aptitudes and propensity of our young associates to eventually become our partners, we cannot leave their gaining the key perspectives and skills to chance. As we have defined the Developer, they are not a discrete element. Instead, they are a complex formula made up of archetypes, skills, knowledge and passion. And it is these archetypes that concern us in Chapters 14 and 16.

The questions that we need to answer are 'How do we apply these archetypical skills within the developer's toolbox?' Think of these as the 'higher' lessons that our Schools are focused on delivering, precisely and efficiently. Our students' futures, the futures of our cities and neighborhoods, the futures of our firms, and

239

even the futures of our wealth depend on how well we perform this task.

As we concern ourselves with the first archetype – The Leader – in this chapter, we face the challenge of bombardment of imagery. Leaders are depicted as heroes, visionaries, and consensus builders. They are men who are above the fray morally and are down in the dirt with their sleeves rolled up when there is work to be done. They slay bears in the wilderness and close deals in the boardroom. And all of this imagery is consistent with our previous descriptions of the developer because the role of developer is inextricable from that of leader.

However, as we recollect these heroic visions of who we are, there are two major hurdles that make this aspect of our education, exceptionally challenging:

1. The feminized corporate culture that permeates our society mocks this imagery. This results in social norms and employment laws that run contrary to the education of the developer as leader. In our mealy-mouthed, politically correct society, not only can you not slay that bear in the wilderness, you cannot even write a terse email without derision. So as we observe the eroding foundations of the 'typical' firms in our industry, we increasingly see that they were built on sand. Our younger organizations were designed to simply act as subservient drones to their institutional equity masters. They churn out profitable junk because they are allowed to.

Because the real men never entered the room and said 'No. There is a better way.' We know that profitability and being excellent are not mutually exclusive – being excellent is just a little bit harder. In order to reestablish our industry en terra firma, we must find bedrock. This is why our firms must be anchored in OUR values and OUR vision and will thrive through OUR cultures of mentorship.

2. The responsibilities that we have conferred upon the leader are not necessarily qualities that we possess – at least not comprehensively. And while we can certainly say that great leaders possess a set of skills that allow them to rise to the challenge, regardless of what it is, truth be told, we may be leaders but not exceptional leaders. From this perspective our skills are buoyed by the fact that we are one of the many parts that are part of that mentorship team, dedicated to our teams' education. It takes a village to build a leader.

As we move forward, it shouldn't come as a surprise that the absolutely critical skills (Leadership and Salesmanship) and Self Awareness are valued, recognized and explored so extensively that entire educations and industries have arisen to teach various theories and debate nuance. Our local bookstores have dedicated sections filled with books that contemplate competing suppositions about and methodologies to define and improve our individual aptitudes in each. More than that, an Amazon.com search will multiply our reading options tenfold, and a Google search will return periodical references, blogs and podcasts that will bury us in material for the rest of our lives. In other words, this landscape is well traversed.

Our goal here is not to claim any authoritarian ground on this subject matter, or to duplicate the efforts of countless experts, PhD's and theoreticians. As such, we will do little to elaborate on the various theories and minutia associated with each (the authors do have some favorites in our reading list in the Appendix). Instead we will focus on our observations and goals as they relate directly to the process of development.

"Management is doing things right; leadership is doing the right things." – Peter Drucker

Leadership. It has already been said a dozen times and in a dozen different ways, that the job of the developer is always to be the leader. In every aspect of our career, we are the 'deciders,' the ones that the entire room looks to when an option must be chosen. This is simply because we are the Owners and therefore the ones taking the risk. The quality of 'leader' is often confused with the role of manager. How could it not be, as we've discussed so many times, since the 'developers' of most organizations are little more than project managers.

But a project manager is primarily an organizer and note-taker. They may pick a direction for the team, and the team may follow it – but they do not inspire the team, they do not provide a vision to the team and compel them to greatness. Among other reasons, that's simply not their job. For our purposes, the project manager is only as valuable to us as the spreadsheet or other resources that they manage. And this is not intended to be an insult. The world needs project managers. It just should not call them developers.

A leader, on the other hand, is *the* expert on the whole project. From the project's inception, he knows what he wants the project to become. He analyzes the critical success factors. He can tell us who will use the product and why. He has intricate knowledge of the building's end-users and their value-sets. He knows how much money they make, and how much money they expect to make in ten years, where they shop, what they drive and why, he can tell us whether or not they wash their cars themselves, and which restaurants they frequent and how often, he knows what they drink at home and when they are out on the town. The leader can tell us who they date and when and if they'll get married.

A leader carefully develops a vision, and carefully assembles his consultants to reach his goals. He conveys the values of the firm and the vision of the project, to the investment committee, debt and equity partners, and every member of the consulting team – from architects and engineers to construction managers and sales or leasing teams. During the design and construction process, he keeps everyone on the team excited and invigorated, and he keeps them *focused* on his vision. And if during the process he decides that the vision needs to change, it is his job to make the alteration.

Within the confines of the project team, he is the field general, the priest, and the parent. The team will look to the developer to know where to go and why, they will look to him to know that it is all going to be ok, and they will look to him for praise and discipline. And this is why the developer must be an adroit leader.

For a leader to be effective at each of these tasks, their knowledge of the industry and its interrelationships must be comprehensive. Becoming an effective leader is a long-term journey that relies on well-honed soft-skills and expert hard ones. It cannot be accomplished in the first year of the program. This is why we spent so much time in the admissions process trying to identify people's propensities to becoming leaders. Depending on their toolbox, it may take five or more years to achieve this goal. From day one however, we begin their training.

Unquestionably, to be able to perform a number of the tasks listed above, an understanding of the progression of the lifecycle of a project is necessary, and level of methodological organization is required – these are all project management skills. Like teaching a child to speak, we begin with object words and lessons, not complete sentences.

[Ross Blaising]

I had an experience that remains with me to this day, in which I was first cognizant of the glaring difference between project management and leadership. I had been hired as a consultant to lead the due diligence efforts (as regarded design and construction implementation) for an ultra-luxury condominium conversion in Boston. The development firm was headquartered in Atlanta.

As we worked through the SWOT analysis, gathered our information and quantified our risks, and worked toward an initial project plan, I found that things were coming together more slowly than I had hoped. As I knew what information I wanted, but was having some challenges getting from my team exactly what I was looking for, I told them what I needed, sent them to Boston, and when they returned, the information I needed was nowhere to be found. With more detail this time, I repeated my process, but the results were the same. The next time, I jumped in and began to do the work myself. I had thought that my team was overwhelmed. So I immediately fell back into the tactical role of just doing the work because I thought that it would be easier and quicker. I'll bet that most of us have done that same thing a hundred times in our careers as leaders.

My boss, the President of the company and an exceptional developer and leader, called me into his office, had me shut the door, and sat me down at his large white marble Saarinen work table. It was replete with stacks of papers, paperclips, and a few pens and highlighters. He said to me, "Ross, I see that you are working on such and such project." I answered that I that my group was not getting the urgency of what I was looking for and thought that it would be easier to get it myself. With a pause, he relaxed back into his chair, collected his thoughts and told me "Your job is to convey to the team exactly what you need and the timeframe in which you need it."

He motioned to the table and its contents that sat between us and began to explain, "Imagine that managing all of this is your job; I have brought you on to manage a $110M acquisition and a $40M construction budget. Your job is to ensure that each of these components" pointing to the contents of the table "is moving in the right direction – where you want them to go. That project [that I was concentrating on] is $100K of $150M. You need to lead the entire table. I don't care if you never 'do' anything. I don't want you 'doing' projects. If you are concentrating on this paperclip, then you are not leading the table and you are not protecting my $150M investment."

Wanting to impress my boss, I left the discussion a little bit crestfallen, but I got it. So that evening I went home and gave the subject considerable thought. He was absolutely correct. I had been hired in a strategic role and had applied a tactical response. Doing this is simply a failure in leadership. What I came to understand is; that if my troops did not understand my message and needs, if they were not invigorated and directed to my goals and vision, then it was not their failure, it was mine. The absence of leadership on my part came from having the wrong focus. I had been so focused on the information that I was trying to assemble, that I forgot that my success was measured by my ability to get my team to do their jobs.

It is within this anecdote that we use two key concepts that illustrate a major deficiency within the world of development. The responsibility of the manager (tactician) and leader (strategist) are distinctly different. They are also very different pay grades. Each of our consultants, our team members, heck, even our financial partners and executive teams, are all there to enable the leader's vision. Each supplies a necessary component of the cake that we are collectively working to bake – but there can still only be one cook in this kitchen. They are our tacticians and we are their leaders. It is this fundamental lack of understanding of roles that we describe throughout the early chapters of this book that has broken down the entire development industry. Lack of leadership on our part has led to the usurpation of control by Wall Street.

In an earlier chapter, while discussing the identification of famous developers, we posited a simple on the streets survey (as we recall the answer would likely be 'The Donald' 95% of the time). If we were to again, employ that methodology and walk out onto the street and ask those same passersby what the key ingredient to leadership is, we would end up with as many answers as the people we asked. There would be little consensus because it is a term used to mean many things, and often a term that is misused.

For most of us, defining leadership is like that famous quote where Supreme Court Justice Potter described the definition of obscenity (pornography): "I shall not today attempt further to define the kinds of material I understand to be embraced within that shorthand description...But I know it when I see it." The majority of people can't describe what 'leadership' is. What they can do however, is identify someone who embodies it. In other words – they know it when they see it.

So if, for the sake of our previous survey, we instead asked the simple question 'Name the most important leader?' more often than not the answer would be the President of the United States. Not surprisingly, because the president is tasked with the role of applying the values of his country and its citizens to the times in which he presides and forming a vision by which to govern. Of course he must 'sell' that vision to the American people and the legislative branch in order to implement it. In times of war, he is tasked with protecting the values the Americans hold dear and guiding his troops' efforts to that end. Our heroes do so with the understanding that they are willing to take and sacrifice their lives for his vision and command.

We all think of the President as the ultimate form of leader because of the scale and consequences associated with his responsibilities. From the birth of our nation, through the end of the twentieth century, we have only given this responsibility to forty-one individuals. And within that exclusive fraternity, there have been only a few who, in the public consciousness, have distinguished themselves as truly outstanding leaders. These include: George Washington, Abraham Lincoln, Theodore Roosevelt, Franklin Roosevelt, John Kennedy, and Ronald Reagan.

Once we step back from the scale of the decisions that our President is tasked to make, there is virtually no difference in the skills that separate a Developer from the President of the United States. On a base level, a leader is a leader and they must deliver the same qualities to their constituents. It is not a coincidence that many of our nation's most beloved leaders have been distinguished war heroes or state governors. The commonalities that have separated the shortlist of leaders above from the rest of their pack are two-fold: Conveyance of Vision and Perseverance in the Face of Adversity or to the completion of important tasks.

Conveyance of Vision. With the exception of perhaps George Washington (who was predisposed to reserved shyness that was often misinterpreted as being aloof), each of the leaders above had excellent oratory skills. They were able to formulate a plan and deliver it to the public in a way that touched the individual and made them feel like they were a part of something greater than themselves. Their greatness came in the way that they addressed the task before them, with a vision based on their values and then (and most importantly) rallied the strength of our Nation by transforming their vision into a shared vision. They presented a new direction.

FDR convinced the nation to allow for the creation of a massive social and economic government overhaul, this to a people who have been historically violently mistrustful of government intervention. Through his speeches and radio broadcast 'fireside chats,' the nation was delivered messages that included: "Confidence...thrives on honesty, on honor, on the sacredness of obligations, on faithful protection and on unselfish performance. Without them it cannot live," or "There is a mysterious cycle in human events. To some generations much is given. Of other generations much is expected. This generation of Americans has a rendezvous with destiny."

As the first President to take full advantage of the television medium, JFK used a similarly populist message when he called upon our citizenry to bond together for great achievements, saying: "And so, my fellow Americans, ask not what your country can do for you; ask what you can do for your country," and "The problems of the world cannot possibly be solved by skeptics or cynics whose horizons are limited by the obvious realities. We need men who can dream of things that never were." JFK challenged us to dream.

After years of unhealed wounds from Vietnam, the embarrassment of corruption in our highest office, and directionless leadership, recession and weak foreign policy, Ronald Reagan was elected to office. His vision coalesced the nation toward strength through a return to our conservative 'bedrock' values, national strength and the eventual defeat of Communism. Reagan's gift was that he could remind us that our destiny as Americans was for greater things than we were aware: "Each generation goes further than the generation preceding it because it stands on the shoulders of that generation. You will have opportunities beyond anything we've ever known." Or, as he said in his farewell address, "I've spoken of the Shining City all my political life. ... In my mind it was a tall, proud city built on rocks stronger than oceans, windswept, God-blessed, and teeming with people of all kinds living in harmony and peace; a city with free ports that hummed with commerce and creativity. And if there had to be city walls, the walls had doors and the doors were open to anyone with the will and the heart to get here. That's how I saw it, and see it still."

Much of what these men achieved, regardless of our individual opinions of the actual achievement, required a message of words that was well placed to touch deeply the recipient. Each leader drew the nation together as a people toward a common goal. Their success came from being inspirational.

In the movie *The American President* there is a short speech where one of the president's advisors (played by Michael J. Fox) argues to the President (played by Michael Douglas) that the people

251

crave leadership: "In the absence of genuine leadership, they'll listen to anyone who steps up to the microphone. They're so thirsty for it they'll crawl through the desert to a mirage and when they discover there is no water, they will drink the sand."

This quote illustrates an important truth – that generally the public will subjugate their individual concerns and beliefs to someone with whom they disagree, if they are confident that the leader has a vision that he honestly believes in. Put differently, people will support a vision with which they might not necessarily agree, if they are confident that that vision is honest and sincere.

Unlike the President of the United States, whose stage is global, the developer has two primary audiences that he must regularly lead and inspire: the external audience and the internal audience. And because they are different, they must each be approached in two very different ways. The external audience is comprised of landowners, communities, government agencies, and end users; whereas the internal audience is comprised of investment committees, debt and equity partners, the project team and construction group.

The External Audience

The external audience is complex and often very difficult to lead. They begin their interaction with the developer from a very mistrustful place. Half of their resentment comes from the facetious caricature of the developers' persona, the lie that the developer always makes tons of money swindling the residents of their neighborhood and created the ugliness and congestion that they see around them. The other half stems from their own fear of change.

Like it or not, we have to overcome each of these on every project that we assemble and entitle. Gaining communities' trust and acquiescence is commonly a daunting task.

During our interaction with the external audience, we can make in-roads or we can build walls. Often the difference comes down to simple choices on our part to include them in the process and incorporate their vision into ours (after all, they will be living with our product long after we are finished and gone). Simple and foolish mistakes can easily derail the efforts, such as pulling up to a community meeting in a Lamborghini, not dressing to our audience, appearing secretive about aspects of our plans, etc.

But most importantly, we will fail to be inspirational to this audience if we cannot find a way to speak to them from that place where they are motivated. Leadership is a reciprocal relationship. What we need to remember is that we are asking this group to trust us, we are asking for them to give us permission to lead them down a path in which they do not necessarily want to travel.

For us to achieve that, they must feel that we are fixing their perceived problems, that we will be respectful of the inconvenience to them that comes with our construction, and that we are honest, open and sincere in our vision. In that way, leadership and mentorship are alike; they are most effective when applied through an outward focus. Sometimes leadership is most effective when those who are being led are unaware of it.

[Robbie Reese]

I recall a situation where Ross and I were exploring the conversion one of our for-sale condominium products to a luxury rental project, in order to accommodate a major change in the economy. The project was in the vicinity of a lot of new, competing class-A apartments. We were under construction and had neither the time, nor the budget to comprehensively redesign the community in a way that would reposition it within the sub-market. I knew that we were in for a bloodbath, given the competition that would also be in lease-up.

So Ross and I chose to concentrate on the redesign within the context of the leasing agents' tour. The experience of renting in our community would already be very positive and the units themselves were very well laid-out and appointed. So our solution was to bring in new interior design talent to concentrate on a leasing office, key corridors (for the tour) and take a fresh look at the models. Rather than choose one of the many local designers that focused on apartment product, we decided to go with a bigger 'name' designer whose expertise was more refined and targeted toward for-sale product.

One of the internal challenges that we faced was a design group that had some fairly strong opinions, who we should be working with and what the project should morph into. I strongly disagreed with their vision, but had to balance our vision with the overall stability of the organization. I felt that it would be better to bring them along, rather than walk over them. While I had never worked with this designer before, Ross had and I had seen his work. So just before going into the meeting, I was well aware of the potential mistrust and struggles that might await. Ross took me aside and said 'just sit back and watch what Mark does here.' Fine, I thought to myself.

Once the meeting began, our designer (who had his own thoughts on the aesthetics of the project) began by listening to our internal design folks as they gave their thoughts and vision for what we must achieve. He listened to every syllable and periodically agreed and praised their thoughts. He showed them that he cared how they felt and that he 'bought-in' to their vision. He knew that they would never be able to 'hear' him until they said everything that was on their minds. Then when it came time for him to speak, he carefully gave them ownership of his own vision by quoting their ideas, and asking questions for which he already had answers. I watched as he bent the internal design team's view to his own and made them feel enthusiastically that it was theirs. It was brilliant. He masterfully led without any indication of leadership. I am often reminded that there are many different paths to successful leadership and sometimes the greatest quality of the leader is to look at the needs of the audience and know which path to take.

Early in the book, as we discussed the Litmus Test, we described a problem that the industry faces in which many developers have ceased to assemble and entitle their own developments. Instead, development firms wait for a broker to do the heavy lifting and put together a package, which is then solicited to the development community. Offers are submitted and negotiated, and the property is finally sold to the highest, most qualified competitor. Obviously this leads to land assemblages which are put together, often in not the best location for us as the developer, and which are at a premium price due to the competition and brokerage fees.

So why is this condition so prevalent? It's very simple: assembling land and entitling it is harder and requires more refined leadership skills. The cost of time and pursuit capital is also at a greater risk. So rather than being better at our jobs, developers have abdicated our roles as the visionary of where we build – to a real estate broker? There is nothing inherently wrong with using the expertise of the broker. The problem arises when the developer no longer directs the broker to *his* goals and *his* locations. Passivity ultimately lessens the competence within our firms. Abdicating vision of location is the exact same thing as abdicating leadership. So even as we utilize a broker to get our land contracts in place, it remains our role to point to the map and say, 'I want this, this and this. Now go get them and we can pay...'

Once we have chosen and secured control of our assemblage, we face a very common challenge: securing the confidence of the stakeholders within that community. Even if we have established a verifiable, twenty-year track record of performing only honest and exemplary work, we always begin at the exact same place with the community. Because there is a fundamental mistrust that the public has for developers, we must constantly hold the same hands, give the same assurances and break down the same walls. It is the developer's job to ask the communities for permission to upgrade their infrastructural system, remove the current ugliness or underutilization of the area, and bring new and necessary amenities that will invigorate the area and stimulate their lives.

Our job is to convince the public that we have a vision that is in their best interest (or better yet, that we are here to implement their vision) and have the talent and resources to implement it. We must effectively convince large groups of mistrustful folks that their trust may be safely placed in us. Like the presidents described above, whose visions were accepted because the message transcended logical descriptions and pictures and instead spoke to their audience in ways that touched them emotionally, the developer's success often relies on our ability to stir the emotions of our constituents and move their passions.

The Internal Audience

Internal leadership on the other hand, is typically a simpler task – or at the very least, differently challenging. Fortunately, those that we are leading internally are already predisposed to work with us, as they are typically hired by us. With them we are already, by definition, the boss. That said, the contractual relationship that we have with our team and consultants will only bring out the very least that it takes to get the job done. If our goal is to get the best that they have to offer, then they too will need to be inspired to our vision.

In Part I of TSORE, we briefly discussed the Matrix organization. We said that matrix organizations were very common in the consulting world, but that they were not generally present in development groups. That is certainly true at the corporate level. At the project level however the structure is almost always a semi-matrix. This is because, especially with mixed-use, virtually every project varies greatly from the next and therefore requires different applications of expertise to achieve the intended goals. When forming our teams, there is also the consideration around balancing the workloads of our consultants. We and they may be making team composition choices based on our pipeline expectations. And while certainly the core project team (partner, associates and accountants) will likely remain constant, the rest of the team may be in flux. Hence the term, semi-matrix.

So within the project team we have two sets of constituents: our core team and our consultants. The core team works with us on a daily basis, knows us intimately and is likely a part of our School for Development. They are motivated by the knowledge and experience that they gain from us and how we are developing their career paths. The rest of the Owner Architect Contractor (OAC) team is another situation altogether.

Earlier in the book we discussed the fact that each trade or profession at the project table thinks that the project is about them; architects think it's an architecture project, contractors think it's a construction project, etc. And this is exactly what we want them to be concentrating on –their role.

But we cannot make the mistake to assume that while they are viewing the project from their own functional perspective, that they have any consideration for the project's overall goals (i.e., the architect may care about the project aesthetics, but he has no interest in the project's profitability). For instance, to get a scarce material that they value, they may suggest putting a key portion of the project on hold for six weeks. They have no visibility, nor incentive to review how the cost of capital for that delay affects the project returns. That is the job of the project leader and his project managers.

The key takeaway is that no matter how much business we give to an individual consultant, when push comes to shove, their primary allegiance is to their firm. And the goal of their firm is to provide us with the most reasonably acceptable solution that requires the least amount of billable time. They are working to pay for their Range Rover, not ours.

That said, we still have the ability to coax from these professionals much more than they are contractually obligated to give. The key to this is internal leadership. While at a pragmatic level, each of these folks is operating out of their own self-interest, more important than that is the fact that each person at the project table has taken a very specific career path. That original motivation comes from a kernel of passion. And finding and speaking to that passion is how we inspire and motivate them. We say this, not at an individual level necessarily, but at least at the level of professional buckets (i.e., architects generally care about…, engineers generally are motivated by…, etc.).

A typical project team consists of engineers, architects, landscape and interior designers, a construction manager, a general contractor, and a sales or leasing team. It is first important to recognize that there is a commonality amongst this group, and that is real estate. They each understand on a basic level, even if they don't necessarily always prefer it, that they are each different slices of the same pie; more specifically – your pie.

That said, each person at the table has chosen a profession that reflects their worldview and that has its own language and structure. This disparity becomes glaringly obvious when we compare our interior designers to our general contractor. Given their druthers, the interior designer doesn't care how much something costs or how long it takes to get, or how difficult it is to install – they only want it to be pretty. On the other hand, the general contractor only cares about how expensive it is (especially in a Lump Sum contract), where they are going to get it, how long it takes to arrive, and what they will need to get it installed. These diametrically opposing worldviews represent the basic 'quality versus cost' tightrope on which we as leaders must direct and balance.

Another glaring difference is the manner in which the two professions operate. The world of design is generally gentle and feelings based, whereas the world of construction is authoritarian. Speaking to a designer in the manner that we would a contractor would be demotivating and hurtful, and speaking to a contractor like we would a designer would result in diminished respect. Yet again, the key to successful leadership is to apply an outward focus to every aspect of our profession. In order to train excellent leaders, we first much teach them to respect every aspect of the project lifecycle. This is because in order to inspire such a diverse team, we need not only to speak their individual languages, but we need to be able to see the art in their work from their perspective.

Leadership Styles

Based on our unique toolbox, and the experiences that we have had, each of us will have our own natural leadership style. We also have an adapted style, which may or may not be congruent with our natural style. Some will be authoritarian, others conciliatory and even others unapparent. None of these are necessarily right or wrong, except in application to the project that we are tasked with leading. And each style may be appropriate at different situations within the same project. Rather than 'right' or 'wrong,' it is better to view leadership from the perspective of appropriate and inappropriate. Ultimately the judgment of the application of our style comes down to 'Did it work? and 'Do people want to continue working with us?' Our evaluation is almost always in arrears. It is therefore best to be adept at as many styles as possible and have as many arrows in our quiver as possible.

A great point for consideration in all aspects of life, but certainly in the application of leadership, is that the lesson that we were all taught by our parents, that 'relationships are 50/50, they are a two-way street' is false. They are not. In fact it is quite the opposite; we are all each 100% responsible for every relationship in our lives. And this most certainly applies to our professional lives.

For instance, we can come home after a hard day at work and see our spouse, who also has had a long, hard day. Because of our respective baggage, our spouse might make an unthinking and uncalled for comment that frankly pisses us off. At that moment, we may react equally nastily; we might ignore it, or we might say, 'Honey, tell me about your day? or 'Go relax, can I get you anything?' In that moment, we are 100% in control of how the rest of our evening unfolds.

This is true in the same way that we are 100% accountable for the projects that we undertake. As such, our relationships with our consultants are actually not reciprocal. We must find a way to be inspired by their work and still understand that they will likely never be inspired by ours. And it's not their job to be. We are the only one at the table that cares about our profit margin – that only inspires us.

Chapter 15

The Allegory of the String and the Bag

"Chaos is the enemy of Order but the enemy of Chaos is also the enemy of Order" – Norman Spinrad

Whenever leadership is discussed, the conversation drifts to the loftier, sexier aspects of the role. We focus on the masculine elements where either a vision is sold to the masses or a leader drops in and takes charge. Leaders are imagined fixing things, or at least providing clarity when the team begins to drift away from achieving the goal. We have also discussed leadership in these very same terms throughout TSORE thus far. And this makes sense because most of us either imagine ourselves as the heroic leader or at least hope to be led by one.

What we must remember is that these instances of decisive leadership are just moments in the process. They are not its entirety. In fact, when it comes to the leader stepping in and 'righting the ship,' these are moments that we never actually want to occur – because they are a result of a failure of leadership. In other words, we fix bad leadership with good leadership.

We have used the example of Winston Churchill as the quintessential leader that forged England into one mind to combat the Nazis in World War II. And while he was the exact right man for the job, his leadership should have been unnecessary. Had Neville Chamberlain not adopted a strategy of appeasement with the Germans leading up to the war, millions of lives could have been saved and WWII not been fought on a continental scale. Churchill's rise to power was the result of a dramatic failure.

So if the heroic leader is necessary at the beginning of the project and occasionally if things drift askew, what should they be doing the other 99% of the time? Well, the answer is simple: they should be leading the team unheroically. In fact, often the best team leadership takes very little obvious 'hands-on' guidance from the leader.

In order to really understand what a leader's real job is, just blur your vision slightly and look at what the leader is actually tasked with: it is simply to maintain equilibrious momentum and remove chaos. Often this is achieved by acting as a counter-balance to the team. Leaders are excellent 'nudgers.' So when we observe the great and booming leadership of Churchill, it was necessary to halt the momentum of a failed strategy and reverse it to achieve a great success. His presence and rhetoric was great because the preceding failure had been great.

Nuance

In the previous chapter, it required little mental gymnastics to understand and accept that the needs of internal and external audiences were unique and that our approach to leading each would need to be equally so. The level of sophistication required for external leadership is different from that of internal leadership, and the successful developer must be master of both.

In addition to the nuance of style and effort required in leading differing audiences, we also must acknowledge that leadership should vary with the complexity of the tasks faced as well. In other words, different tasks must be managed differently. Of course we are all saying to ourselves: 'this is pretty obvious.' And while it is not a particularly brilliant concept, it is one that most leaders fail to consciously enact. And this is because we, as leaders, often fall into the lazy trap of using the same gear for every challenge.

For example, consider the 'micro-manager.' We've all had to deal with one at some point in our careers. We may have even been one. But we definitely all know that guy; no matter what the task, they are over-the-top commanding in their rhetoric, checking up on our progress every 15 minutes, demanding that we explain each step of how we intend to succeed at the task, and not unoccasionally, combative in their demeanor. They generally make us feel like they think that we're incompetent. And while being very hands-on is sometimes necessary, consistent micro-management is an acknowledgement of a failure of leadership. It occurs for a few basic reasons:

1. They have not constructed the right team for the job.
2. They have not provided the appropriate vision to the team.
3. They conflate leadership with control.

Or more often than not,

4. They lack confidence in their own abilities, which does not allow them to trust in the abilities of their team.

Regardless of the driver of this behavior, the micro-manager may complete tasks on time and on budget, but that success is often offset by the unintended chaos that they cause by demoralizing their team. A micro-manager may get adequate results, but they rarely get the best results from their team because they show them a lack of respect. Micro-managers tend to have a single gear in an industry that requires them to have ten.

While there are multiple caricatures of failing leadership types, we use the micro-manager above simply because of its prevalence. Our leaders, our developers must be multi-faceted in their skills and approach.

The (un)Hero

Returning to our concept of unheroic leadership, which is that space that consists of the majority of the actual time dedicated to leading, our actions must remain consistently leader-like. So what are we actually doing in that space? We know that it is more than just management. Certainly there is considerable critical thinking. There is mentorship. There is continuing to focus each member on their immediate goals. There is reminding the team of the collective goal. There is energizing and reprimanding, and of course helpful nudging.

From a high-level, all of these activities coalesce into a single initiative: the limiting of chaos. After all, it is chaos that is the enemy of all projects. During the regular course of any effort, it is the leader who stands above the team with a very large umbrella, protecting them from any potential chaos that might rain down upon them.

That chaos may come the outside or from within the team itself. This is why leaders must be adept at always managing the big picture. And truthfully, excellent leaders also retain the ability to zoom-in from the macro to the micro pictures. There is a spectacular scene in John Hughes' beloved film *Ferris Bueller's Day Off* that takes place at the Art Institute of Chicago. In the scene, Cameron stands in front of the great pointillist painting 'Sunday Afternoon on the Island of Le Grande Jatte' by George Seurat. In the first shot, we can take in the entire painting as well as the wall on which it is placed. In a series of successive stills, we zoom in step after step until the entire painting morphs from a beautiful beach scene to a series of overlapping stipples of color.

The developer must not only ensure that the building gets built, but he must also verify that the door handles are appropriate for aesthetic, cost and availability. Leadership, in the context of real estate development, is a constant and dynamic flow of shifting perspectives that the developer must be adept at leading.

One of the ways that the leader shields the team from chaos is by segregating, assigning and managing tasks in a manner appropriate to their complexity and importance to the goals of the effort. We can distill tasks into two types:

1. Those that have fairly straightforward goals and should be reproduced exactly, time after time. These tasks thrive on efficiency and consistent reproducibility, and

2. Those that require creative solutions. These tasks often have a defined starting point and a general ending point, with a semi-uncertain path in between.

It is at this point that we introduce two new management theories; theories that differentiate between the two dichotomies above and that marry our concept of limiting or controlling chaos. We have entitled these 'string theory' and 'bag theory.'

The String. We call activities that are regular and consistently reproducible 'string tasks' and apply a methodology we have correspondingly entitled 'string theory.' String tasks tend to be simple (not necessarily easy), but definable and lacking complexity. Some common string activities would include internal document organization, payroll issues, municipal filings, etc. For these tasks, imagine that we have a string that is pulled taut and at each end is fixed to two opposing walls. Suspended on that string is a disk or ball, which may be slid to the left or the right, as the disk is either pulled or pushed (like with an abacus). The task consists of moving the disk from one point to the other. It is simple, efficient and the result is the same each time the task is performed.

Success of string projects is generally assumed. Often they require less sophisticated skill sets to complete (or at least more narrow bands of expertise). Because they are regularly reproduced, the completion of these tasks may be regimented and performed with tight systems or restrictions. String tasks tend to be highly *process* driven. Therefore we address them by strictly defining the process by which they are completed. Once this is achieved, they are easily managed. Accuracy is increased and time is saved.

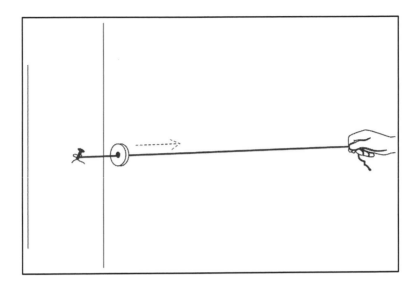

Figure 8. Illustration of String Theory

The Bag. Once we have removed those simple tasks and initiatives from the totality of responsibilities on any given development project, we are still left with a tremendous amount of work to be done. These remaining items, which may comprise upwards of 70% of the preliminary phases of work, are the more complicated efforts. We describe them as complicated because the developer often begins with only a fuzzy vision of the resulting product. Clear solutions will require the creativity of the team to complete.

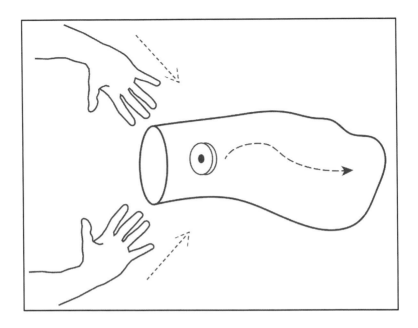

Figure 9. Illustration of Bag Theory

It is pretty simple to understand why a different system of team management would be required for creative efforts. Using the example of the string above, we had a fixed beginning point and a fixed ending point. These two bookends define the path of the string and allow it to be pulled taut. This allowed the task (disc) to slide effortlessly toward the solution. With a creative effort we have only one fixed point (where we are now).

Even if we know some things about where we are going (i.e., there will be 300 units, it will be four stories tall, there will be a pool and leasing office), this tells us virtually nothing consequential about the end product. In fact, if we described those guiding points to an architect, an engineer and a contractor, and then asked them to draw the final product, the resulting drawings would likely have very little in common.

Through the creative process, all of our visions coalesce. And therefore, with only one fixed point, our tightly regimented, process driven string would hang flaccid against the wall.

For simplicity sake, the components of bag theory are as follows:

- The bag = order and organization
- The ball = the project
- The liquid = the project team
- The pressure = vision, program, schedule, vision…

Creative team leadership requires a different device, which we call 'the bag.' To understand the concept of 'bag leadership' or 'bag theory,' imagine that we now have a transparent, oblong plastic bag that is completely filled with a clear liquid and a small ball or disc (similar to the one used in the string above). As with the string theory, our goal is to move the ball from one end of the bag to the other. The difference, of course is that because the ball is suspended within the bag, it is impossible to be grabbed or pushed or pulled.

Our fingers can never actually touch the ball. So rather than applying direct, process-driven pressure, we must coax the ball in the right direction by placing indirect pressures on the bag. When leading a highly creative team, the tools we can use to apply that pressure include the developer's vision, timeline or schedule, product typology and program, aesthetics and budget. In a creative environment, we know where the ball must end up; however, its path is uncertain.

Harnessing Creativity and Limiting Chaos

We can easily distill the principles in our string and bag theories into direct versus indirect leadership. And thus far we have discussed them in terms getting the best results from the teams that we are leading. We have discussed these components in terms of managing a project. These exact same theories should be applied to the operation of the School for Development and the growth of the individual as well.

1. At the project level, we understand that creativity is a force that can be highly powerful when harnessed or incredibly stagnant or misdirected when left without limits. The bag becomes our creative space. However, that creative space is most effective when unencumbered by the more simplistic tasks. Through segregation of the two, we are able to maximize the effectiveness of each. Therefore, the bag and the string are mutually reliant.

2. When these theories are applied at the organizational level, the purpose shifts from harnessing creativity back to the initial discussion in this chapter of limiting chaos. Our goal here is to remove the forces which can be defocusing to the development and learning processes. We have all seen throughout our careers that the issues that most directly derail a smooth office environment have little to do with the actual activities of development. Without discussing them in the context of a string or bag, we have already put forth important principles and maxims that are intended to limit short- and long-term

chaos. Whether this is promoting our values to our prospective students or overhauling our hiring process, we seek to limit employee turnover. In chapter 17, we will explore a number of other principles that allow us to limit and control the chaos at the enterprise level. These each will rely upon removing strings to create an effective bag.

3. The final level upon which these theories work is the individual. As we know, leadership is a very complex skill to develop. By incorporating the language of the string and the bag into the daily operations of the firm and the projects we undertake, we create a mnemonic device for our students. This visual image reinforces their ability and desire to look at complex goals and quickly separate them into smaller, achievable parts. And whether those parts are simple versus complex, rote versus creative, or significant versus trivial, we reinforce a methodology for critical thinking which works to increase the capacity of their natural leadership toolboxes. If we succeed in this task, we are 70% of the way toward achieving our goal.

Chapter 16

Archetype II – The Salesman

*"Don't be so modest. You always started too low. Walk in
with a big laugh. Don't look worried. Start off with a couple
of good stories to lighten things up. It's not what you say, it's
how you say it – because personality always wins the day."*
– Willy Loman, Death of a Salesman, Act I

The second half of the discussion of the developer's primary
toolbox skills relates to the Archetype of The Salesman. We have all
heard the line 'Everything you do is selling,' which is both true and
untrue…but in either case contains at least a gross
oversimplification. For people with a career in sales, that is a filter
through which they view the world. To them experience is
transactional.

And again, there is some truth in that. Each morning we wake up
and select an ensemble of clothes to convey a product that we market
and sell to our peers and the world. We sell the product of our firm
throughout the day to an array of landowners, vendors and fellow
developers. At night, we use sales to close the pretty girl at the bar.
Through the very nature of our responsibilities, the real estate
developer is inextricably linked to the salesman.

But while we share their DNA, we are not necessarily salesmen
in the way that they are salesmen, or in the way that you might think.
So we can begin this exploration with the exact same question
posited in the opening of chapter 14, 'How do we apply these
archetypical skills within the developer's toolbox?'

Salesmanship. We've already shouted it from the mountaintops: 'Developers are simply salesmen' and as such; it is not a huge leap of logic that the second critical skill that our associates must master is salesmanship. That said, the authors have not been entirely forthright in our proclamation. We're not really technically salesmen, but more specifically we are the salesman's first cousin, the marketer. In case anyone is asking, *Well, if we are marketers, then why in the world did you say for the last 150 pages that we were salesmen?* There are a few answers to this question, the most truthful of which is that to say that 'we are marketers' sounds really clunky. The second answer is that most people don't know the difference. And the third answer is that this dichotomy gives us a pretty good introductory paragraph.

Sales vs. Marketing. There are over a thousand books in print on the subject of marketing, and not surprisingly there are a number of definitions for the concept. The American Marketing Association defines marketing as "the activity, set of institutions, and processes for creating, communicating, delivering, and exchanging offerings that have value for customers, clients, partners, and society at large." On the other hand, the Chartered Institute of Marketing defines marketing as "The management process responsible for identifying, anticipating and satisfying customer requirements profitably." For our purposes as development firms, the definition is:

"Marketing is the art of identifying the customer, keeping the customer and satisfying the customer."

Sales, on the other hand, is a component of the marketing process. Successful marketing culminates in a sale. Often however, when we think of sales, we think of a financial transaction. In that way, we are not really salesmen at all. After all, when do WE actually ever sell anything? We are definitely consumers. We purchase land, equity, debt, labor, materials – we even purchase salesmen. We commonly 'close the buy,' but from a 'closing the sale' perspective (defined by the disposition of a building), we tend to hire that out to salespeople (i.e., brokers, leasing agents). In some cases our firm may own an in-house brokerage, but even then the actual sales transaction of a property is rarely physically managed by the developer.

And yet we say that we're salesmen? Yes, it is true. For this to make sense, we need to separate the definition of 'sales' from the concept of a 'financial' conveyance. Because, what we developers are selling is not tangible, we are selling the concepts of trust and confidence.

When do we market? Everything that our new organization does has a marketing component. When we established our organization as a 'values based' 'school for development,' we created a product. When we convey that to the world, we are marketing who we truly are. As we train our associates, we are creating marketing instruments for that product.

Each building that we create is a tangible testament to our espoused values. To our communities, we market our appropriateness and quality. To our equity partners and debt providers, we market our quality and stability. To our end-users, we market our understanding of their needs and our quality. To our associates, we market our dedication to their growth and the quality of our mentorship programs. All of these marketing moments are a singular extension of our values that are illustrated through varying manifestations.

One of the key components that an associate must learn is that for as long as they are members of our program, they are marketing components of 'us.' And not until they establish their own firms do they ever represent themselves. So until that time, whether the activity involves purchasing or assembling property, leading or participating on a project team, participating on charitable boards or in community organizations, being respectful to coworkers and family, making charitable donations, and so on, we build and reinforce a reputation that is an extension of our firm's values.

How we act is the embodiment of 'who we are.' It is the most important part of our marketing. As Benjamin Franklin famously said, "It takes many good deeds to build a good reputation, and only one bad one to lose it." Therefore it is incumbent on us as leaders to also live up to the values that our firm's espouse. Which is why it is so critical that during the inception of our firms the entire leadership team gives careful thought and reaches agreement as to which values will comprise that list. We are designing our own shackles.

So then when are we salesmen? There are hurdles that we must cross in every project lifecycle in which we need to cash-in on some of our marketing efforts; in these transactions we are salesmen. We can think of these moments as a mortgage on our reputations. When we ask our community stakeholders to trust us to alter their neighborhood, when we sit down with our equity partners or bankers, etc., it is then that we are salesmen. And we had better be good ones. Because of the scale of the projects that we undertake and the intense investment of pursuit time and capital we must 'close' the sale 100% of the time. And yet, while the 'sale' is not the most important part of the marketing process, it is the most critical part.

[Ross Blaising]

When I really started to develop and refine my presentation skills, I was eighteen and a freshman in college. As the prior product of a public school education, I had delivered a few book report presentations in front of my classmates, always accompanied by the usual terror that feeds the nightmares of children everywhere. Even though I knew everyone in the class, my confidence was low and demeanor was nervous and stiff. Fortunately, I was articulate and could write compellingly. I could read my words from my seat without trepidation. However the moment that I moved to the front of the class, my legs became Jell-O.

Because I had chosen to pursue a degree in architecture, I was regularly forced to confront these fears and develop them into strength. One reason for this is that the design portion of an architectural education requires almost weekly presentations. These 'critiques' as they are called may be in front of 6 or 16 or 60 people, depending on the day.

There is also an added presentation twist that comes with art or architecture presentations, which is that the subject matter is personal to the designer. We are presenting something that we created. Because the audience is interactive (asking questions and offering criticism), the designer is also forced to learn to withstand being publically challenged, but also to compellingly defend our ideas and vision. In this way, the experience is excellent preparation for one of the developer's greatest key success factors.

Personally, I noticed a major shift in my abilities in my second year of undergrad when I was suddenly comfortable enough not to get rattled by these very public jousting matches. I found myself giving me permission to be myself. I found my natural style, which is a mixture of formal and casual traits, and let it flow freely.

Now, the energy that I feel before speaking to a crowd is excitement and not fear. I regularly make jokes and give tangential anecdotes in an attempt to engage the crowd and put them at ease so that they can actually 'hear my vision' and interact with me. Of course there are always the particularly hostile or obtuse groups. For them I try to change the tempo and cadence of the discussion. I sometimes poke gentle fun at the crazies in the room – or even at myself. This is to break down the negative energy of the group.

The goal is to have the mob to acquiesce to me as the leader. As we've said, leadership is a mutual relationship and if we cannot get the crowd to cede control, we cannot get them to hear us. And that actually happens sometimes. In that case, I try to find a way to terminate the discussion and get out of there. Live to fight another day. Winning support is a war and not a single battle.

Another thing that I have found to be very useful is to have someone who I trust and is also a good presenter there with me as a partner. Someone who can watch the crowd and if I start to go down a bad path or get into trouble, he can jump in and take over. And then working together as a team, we can jump back and forth, alternating as presenter and crowd watcher. This sort of strategy, when performed

> seamlessly, has the similar effect of taking the crowd off balance and lowering their inhibitions. My coauthor Robbie and I tend to work very well in this capacity.

Self Awareness. When I [Blaising] was young, a good friend of mine helped put my ego in check, when he responded to one of my self-aggrandizing rants by nodding his head and saying very casually, "You know, we all believe things about ourselves that aren't true." This is probably one of the most accurate statements that I've ever heard – certainly about myself. In fact, while to one extent or other, everyone is susceptible to falling victim to the deadly sin of pride, the real estate developer is in particular peril.

We described in earlier chapters how the real estate developer is very vulnerable to eventually falling for their own sales pitch. It is a condition that is probably very similar to the 'god complex' that is sometimes described in surgeons where, because of their immediate control of life or death in their patients, they come to believe that they can accomplish more than is humanly possible or that their opinion is automatically above those with whom they may disagree. It is an acute form of narcissism.

Whereas the surgeon's actions have an immediate and direct effect on their patients' lives, the real estate developer has a similar effect on our communities. He envisions a different reality for a space, designs and funds the change, and then risks his firm's and in part his families' security to realize that vision. And he does this repeatedly. This combination of risk and control is not present in most professions. It requires a tremendous ego to change the world.

That said, the unchecked ego leads to bad decisions, gambling and eventually a lack of respect for the forces that guide our profession. And this is why, during their education in our programs, we must interject both humility and self-awareness into our associates' lives. Who knows, it might be therapeutic for us as well. But the way in which we impress upon someone simultaneously that they are both a Master of the Universe and also quite fallible is definitely one of the great challenges that we face.

Unlike other parts of our mentorship program, it is almost impossible to provide a recipe for successful self-awareness. Each associate is different and the conditions of their program will be equally unique. They may have many areas in life and in their profession where they excel and are prideful. The educational program, in which they are enrolled, may be design to foster healthy competitiveness in which the teams thrive on the energy of being better that their peers.

There are many examples in sports where entire teams feed off of the positive energy of one of a few, or an individual uses their own self-confidence to propel themselves to victory. One of the most prominent of these stars is John McEnroe, whose ego and tantrums on the court became infamous. McEnroe channeled his outbursts of this energy to out-psych and upset his opponents and to focus his own energy on producing some of the most amazing tennis shots ever captured on film.

Continuing with McEnroe as the example, there is also a very evident danger to a culture which is too highly charged with competitiveness or that overly celebrates triumphs. There can be surprisingly fine lines between confidence and arrogance and conceit. More important to the organization is the effect that these perceptions have to the groups as a whole. Generally speaking, confidence is celebrated, arrogance is tolerated and conceit is held in contempt. As leaders of our organizations, we must balance the development of the individual with the needs of the organization as a whole.

We have discussed at length in previous chapters the concept that, due to the energy and egos that are inherent and sometimes necessary within the development team, physical separation is recommended. Clearly the authors believe that promoting healthy levels of confidence is a necessary component to a highly performing development team; however it is up to each organization to establish the norms for their individual culture. We have said the good development teams are inherently unstable and certainly ego adds a fair portion of that instability.

Once established, a challenge for the mentors is to identify and address behaviors that are outside the tolerance of the organization. Some of the behaviors that can indicate a lack of self-awareness include:

- Real mean-spiritedness in boasting.

- Associates becoming prideful of successes that were not theirs.
- Unhealthy tension within the teams.
- Unflattering feedback from outside of the organization (public).
- Behaviors that could be harmful to others.

The goal of our programs is to methodically turn each Associate into the best version of the person and real estate developer that they can be. That process involves more than teaching them lessons about finance and project management. We must build up their egos and be their greatest cheerleaders, but also be the guiding 'hands of reason' that temper their impulses to spin off the face of the planet. Helping them to achieve the necessary controls and limits to their egos is one of the most intense areas of our program. It is a goal in which success relies on their receiving good mentorship. This is because building our associates as people requires a very personal touch.

To achieve our goal we must remember that we are not trying to turn them into clones of us. This makes it incumbent on us to really be aware of their toolbox and to regularly monitor it, and then to convey our findings and beliefs to them. Throughout their six years in our program, a very hands-on approach not only to 'what they know,' but more importantly to 'who they are' is necessary. Our program and our firms are 'values based.'

So without being paternalistic in the approach, we must think of these young folks as our family. We must teach them how to view the world. We must give them all the lessons necessary so that they can one day, go out into the world and do for others what we have done for them. Effectively, as we said earlier, we 'need to teach them to shave the right way.'

Hopefully it remains clear that the keys to the long-term success of our young associates lies in qualities that are outside of the natural education provided within 'typical' firms that currently comprise our industry. These most critical skills upon which the success of the developer relies simply cannot be taught by an industry that is focused primarily on hard skills. And we see the results of turning our profession over to their project managers.

Hiring for and teaching hard skills is like having our future generations memorize lists of nouns and verbs and nothing else. While these both comprise valuable parts of our language, they are incomplete. We are unable to structure a sentence or convey a thought. The focus on the soft skills of leadership, salesmanship and self-awareness provides our students with articles and conjunctions that augment their vernacular and leave us and the world with fluent developers.

Chapter 17

Stability

"The minotaur more than justifies the existence of the labyrinth." – Jorge Luis Borges

As we have progressed through TSORE, we have constantly discussed change. The industry has changed as power has shifted from the developer to the banker. The way that we view ourselves must change. How we structure our firms must change. Who we hire must change. How we hire them must change. How we train them must change. When put together, all of this could seem daunting. It really doesn't have to be.

In fact, that is why we structured this book into two distinct parts, with the first dedicated to the strategic objective of changing our mindsets and the latter focused on the more tactical subject matter of how we implement it. Regardless of whether the modification springs from the earlier or latter chapters, they should fold together seamlessly. The goal is to reintroduce a level of structural integrity to our firms in which each of the parts (intentions, goals, actions and outcomes) are aligned and supportive of our consistent success.

Although we have discussed the various components of our metamorphosis in a myriad of ways, when abstracted, they serve the singular purpose of creating stability through the elimination of chaos. In this way, there is little distinction between reinvigoration of our passion for our profession, reassessing our values, being more selective in our choice of projects, adjusting our methods of hiring and training and ultimately operating our firms.

Each of our major efforts should, at their core, incorporate a component limiting chaos. The most direct way that we addressed this topic was with *the string* and *the bag* in chapter 15. In that particular case, our context was with the leadership of a team or a project. Those same principals apply to the day-to-day governance of our firm.

As the leading mentors in our Schools for Development, we must acknowledge that chaos may enter our teams from the most innocuous of areas. This is true whether our organization is a small development company or a part of a larger, more comprehensive real estate services umbrella. It is however now that the point that we have made regarding the separate placement of the development group within the organization receives its fullest expression.

We are hopefully in agreement that a highly performing development company is comprised of personalities that have a greater level of instability than a highly effective accounting team or expert construction group or property management organization. If our experience is within a large, multi-faceted organization, we might be inclined to make the argument that 'Our teams operate next to each other right now and we don't have a problem.' On the surface, this may or may not appear true. But we have to remember that it is most likely that we don't have a group of *developers* right now – at least not as is defined in this text. What we have is a group of project managers. Once we acquire the *right* folks, and begin to treat and train them under different rules than the rest of the organization, the clash will emerge and it will add chaos to every part of the company that it touches.

Because the culture of a development group is creative, unique and often boundary pushing, our job as leaders is to balance that organization with the necessary stability that allows for the instability to remain highly productive. In other words, we must infuse the development group with limits and boundaries – just different ones than the rest of the organization. If we attempt to establish two sets of behavioral rules for different individuals operating within the same fishbowl, we will invariably end up in an Orwellian dilemma. "All animals are equal, but some animals are more equal than others."

Every corporate environment has a series of factors that are common to all organizations, regardless of their location or profession. While each company may answer or address them differently, they are issues that we know will always be addressed. And addressing them means putting in place a series of policies intended to bring a normalization to the expectations of their employees and which gives them standards and comfort, thereby reducing chaos.

One of the things that we will find is that most interoffice and operational issues are fairly stable. See Figure 10 below.

The Typical Organization	Stable	Chaotic
Office space	•	
Work hours	•	
IT, Cell phones and support	•	
Pay periods	•	
Pay scales		•
Bonus		•
Job title and promotions		•
Vacation	•	
Project goals	•	
Special projects		•
Education		•

Figure 10. Typical Stability and Chaos within an Organization

That said, *fairly stable* does not necessarily optimize the effectiveness of the team. Our goal is to remove as much of the potential chaos as possible. Therefore having a policy is better than not, but having the best policy to support the personalities of the specific team is and must be the goal of a TSORE organization.

As we review Figure 10, many of the supporting tools are placed in the stable column, meaning that they can be regularly counted upon. These enhance, rather than distract from the purposes of the Company. So for instance, when we say that the office space is stable, we mean that employees know where they are supposed to arrive to perform their jobs on a daily basis. And when we refer to work hours, most employees know at what time they should arrive at the office. These are not dynamic issues within the daily operation of the company.

A category which could, through no fault of the organization, vacillate between static and dynamic would be the IT / Cell Phone category. On a typical day, everyone's IT products (laptops, software, servers, cell phones) work without error and the environment is static. Chaos enters the organization when one of these devices breaks down. The magnitude of chaos will be related to:

1. How critical the device is at the time of the defect.
2. How often breakdowns occur.
3. Overall impression of the quality of the equipment within the office.

That third item may be the most difficult to contend with because there is not necessarily any link between the reality of the situation and the impression that those in the office hold of the situation.

Regardless, at the point of defect, a very reliable and stable tool becomes a chaotic issue, which results immediately in a decrease in productivity. How well we are prepared will determine the extent of the effects of that chaos. For instance, if it is a critical tool that breaks down often and there is not a ready solution, the chaos may initially destroy the productivity of the individual and then, through complaints and general office sniping, spread to the entire team. If on the other hand, there is an in-house IT department or external consultant at the ready, the chaos may be isolated and contained. If there is a back-up device to provide the employee, the chaos may be totally reduced to the point of inconsequence.

Our goal is to understand which issues within the firm contribute (even remotely) to potential chaos in our students' lives. If a little preparation on our part allows us to move a chaotic item to the 'stable' column, we have effectively removed a portion of the unproductive stress from their minds, thereby making our creative and learning efforts more productive (i.e., higher performing).

This is effectively, our underlying theme of stability or 'controlled chaos.' And how do we add the stability? The answer is simple. Chaos is controlled by removing the unnecessary chaos. This is effectively the string and bag approach applied to the daily operations of the firm.

As with many of the topics, lists and materials contained in this book, our caveat that 'Each and every organization is unique to its own values, goals, product type, region, partner skills, etc.' continues to apply. Figure 10 is only a brief, non-exhaustive example. It does however, contain some of the most common and egregious examples of issues which are not typically viewed as consequential by the leadership team, but which contribute an inordinate amount of chaos to the team dynamics and effectiveness.

Critical Chaotic Issues

As we progress through the following topics, we will be addressing some issues that are often not recognized as potential problems. They go unaddressed within our firms, and when the chaos does appear, it is often not attributed to these overlying themes. Instead blame is attributed to the individual and not the actual driver of chaos. The improvements that we make can be categorized as 'incremental improvements.' Don't let that detract from their importance.

Our fast-paced culture does not often hold up incrementalization in high regard. Magazine articles are more often geared toward rags to riches stories. Our eyes tend to focus on charts that 'hockey-stick' rather than plod along northward. We root for the hare over the tortoise. In part, that may be because there is nothing sexy about long-term planning and methodical implementation. That said, there is a colossal value to the stability of manageable growth- and limited chaos. And within our daily bombardment of the new, the fresh and the sexy, there do exist certain examples of business plans that revolutionize through incremental improvement.

We all recall from B-school, the case study of 3M, which is famous for their approach to incremental progress with products; the most famous of which is the Post-It note. The story has become legendary. However, more in-line with our subject matter is the rockstar in the re-imagination and incremental improvement category: Dyson.

The Dyson approach has been to take a commonplace item and re-engineer it for much greater utility. Whether it was pioneering bagless waste collection, or increasing power and suction through their cyclone technology, or increasing maneuverability through their 'ball' technology, Dyson has revolutionized an otherwise stagnant and boring product sector. The Dyson vacuums don't necessarily do anything that their competitors don't do, they just do everything a bit better. And when it comes to limiting the potential chaos within our firms, we too can do things just a bit better.

Title. As was previously discussed under the topic of the typical developers' career path, there are a series of titles that are commonplace within our industry. These include: Analyst, Development Associate, Project Manager, Development Manager, Developer, Development Director, Vice President of Development, City Partner, State Partner, Regional Partner, Partner. Sometimes they are even further fine-tuned with designations of 'executive,' 'junior' or 'senior.' And most likely, each of us has held at least three. The actual title may seem innocuous because our jobs were the same, regardless of what we were called. However these seemingly irrelevant distinctions on what we are called do have very real psychological effects on the entire team's pride, frustration, cohesiveness or fractiousness.

We all know that people use their title to establish a comfort-zone as to their place in the corporate hierarchy. People negotiate for titles when getting hired. Internally, titles typically do more harm than good because they are used as tools to divide rather than unite. And while they are neither inherently good or bad, the tool that is intended to create stability externally can very easily become a wedge of chaos internally.

So when we think about titles, we need to ask two basic questions:

1. For whom is the title intended to communicate?

2. Does the title convey any information that is standardized
   within the industry?

As to the first question, we need to return to the theme of an
'outward focus versus inward focus' that has been applied to almost
every subject in the book. A title that speaks exclusively to an
internal hierarchy is irrelevant. We don't actually need to convey
anything internally. In other words, if the title does not convey
something that is materially important to the client or project team,
then it is nonsensical and chaotic. Additionally, due to the relative
small size of all development teams, 'executive,' 'junior' and
'senior' designations are always irrelevant.

The second question, 'Does the title convey any information that
is standardized within the industry?', can also be problematic for
developers. The reason is that, other than perhaps Partner, the titles
above don't actually convey anything of significance. This is for two
reasons; the first is that there aren't any defined skill levels that are
consistently applied to each title across the industry, and second
because the titles are not even standardized from firm to firm. In
fact, the only reason that 'Partner' is a real title is because it
consistently denotes a situation where the individual is tasked with
deal generation and implies both ownership in the organization or
deal as well as assuming a level of invested risk.

As developers move from firm to firm throughout their careers,
they acquire some form of logical or illogical collection of the above
listed titles. In theory, these titles are reflective of specific skills and
experience. Unfortunately, this is only 'in theory,' as without

standardization, titles remain opaque when it comes to illuminating skills.

Among the many advantages of the system we propose, ascertaining the experience-level of a prospective employee no longer occurs. This is of course because our model is based on consistently hiring entry level Associates and methodically growing them into Partners.

The TSORE strategy completely averts the 'title to skill-level' chaos by stripping all of the extraneous titles from the organization and adopting a very simple model. Of course there remain the necessary Partner and Executive Team titles. However, when hired, our new student becomes an employee and receives the title of Associate (or more specifically Associate, 1st Year). They progress through the six years of our programs with the only title differentiator being the suffix. At the end of their education in our programs, they are offered the position of Partner. Under this system, there is no political jockeying for title or no undercurrent of animosity about who deserves what. It's really that simple to lift a weight from our firms and from their minds, and to limit the wrong stress and competition from the organization.

If this proposal sounds radical, it is because it is not a system typically applied to our profession. That said, one profession we deal with every day has clearly resolved these issues. Perhaps the cleanest model to consider for the development world is with our legal brethren. In a law firm there are Associates and there are Partners (for our purposes, disregard the 'Of Counsel' stepchild). When we are curious and inquire about the level of experience of the Associate working on our behalf, they will answer will the number of years they have been an Associate (i.e., 'I'm a third year Associate.').

Business Cards. Associated with the subject of title is the business card. Here we return to the question 'For whom is the title intended to communicate?' We should come to the exact same answer here as we did with the question of title above. The business card is an outwardly focused tool that conveys contact information to its recipient; presumably a landowner, municipality, vendor, or debt or equity partner.

Accordingly, what we propose here is that the only titles expressed on your business cards are for the Partner level or the C-Suite. If however, due to the design and layout of the business card, it looks bare without titles, then the title of Associate (sans year suffix) could be added.

One industry that has wholly embraced the confusion of the title and its placement on a business card is the commercial side of the banking industry. Every banker seems to be a Vice President, no matter their age or experience level. How can this be? Not only that, they have some Vice President title variant that means absolutely nothing to the recipient of the business card; Junior VP, Senior VP, First VP, Second VP, Managing VP, etc. What does this mean? Why do we care? Is a First VP a higher or lower level than a Second VP?

We might even be inclined to ask for clarification if it weren't for the fact that the answer could not even be accidentally interesting or useful. All that we know for sure, when we receive a lender's business card is that it was not designed with us (the client) in mind. It is just a self-serving internal status symbol that we could frankly care less about. Commercial banking is a glaring example of an industry that would benefit from our shift of focus from inward to outward.

Compensation Package. Within the development world, the ambiguity that affected the issue of job titles above is also apparent when we survey the compensation package structures from one firm to the next. We do recognize that in a market economy standardization at an industry level makes no sense. Each market and development firm is its own unique snowflake. Some are more entrepreneurial than others. Some are tied to specific equity and ownership structures that limit forms of compensation. Some firms are specialists such that they work best when those responsible for certain aspects of a project are rewarded over others.

However, there is a great opportunity, under our Associate system, to standardize compensation within the firm. For instance, it is ridiculous to have one Associate, 2nd year earning $58K per year and another earning $62K.

When we approach the subject of compensation, we should remember that it is intended to be a tool for creating employment stability within the organization. It is also an opportunity for a firm to reward the behaviors that it wants to promote. There is really nothing more to it. The compensation package consists of a fairly standardized kit of parts, which include salary, bonuses, benefits and other incentives.

It is fascinating to see how often the compensation package is misused to an extent that it results in the chaos of employment turnover, internal rivalry and general discontentment. This misapplication and misalignment of the compensation package is most often a result of a misunderstanding of or lack of respect for the tools themselves. TSORE firms should never face these problems.

Salary. The first and most basic tool in the compensation package is salary. Often, sophisticated development firms have established both job descriptions and pay scale ranges for each job title within the firm, while many smaller firms are looser in their approach. From the firm's leadership or hiring manager's perspective, the salary range gives them the opportunity to have some leeway to entice an applicant if more than one company is competing for the candidate.

The problem with a pay range is the fallacy of secrets. Invariably, each person's individual pay becomes public knowledge and employees not at the top of the pay scale become resentful. Even if the delta is only a thousand or two dollars. Once the differences are known and disseminated throughout the team, each member finds a reason that they should be the highest-paid person, or at least higher than one of their co-workers. It could be because they have been there longer, or they think that they are smarter, or work harder, or have been part of a more important project, etc. Then they begin to worry that they are not valued by their bosses as much as someone else. The fact is that there is no upside to the organization having a pay range.

Clearly we bring all of this unnecessary chaos upon ourselves, but why? It certainly isn't fun or efficient to spend our time putting out unnecessary fires. Nor is it enjoyable to weaken the culture of our organizations. It isn't soothing, nor does it give us the confidence to take more vacations or get more enjoyment from our private lives. The answer is that the salary range is the result of an inward focus, which we perpetuate by not challenging the premise. It was used in our previous firms and it's what we do naturally.

Rather than continuing this potentially chaotic system in our organization the six-year mentorship model that our program creates effectively removes the constancy for that competition and bifurcates it to the beginning (initial hire) and the end (completion) of the program. It establishes (and potentially publishes) our six-year pay schedule for Associates. This way, everyone knows what they and their fellow Associates earn. Additionally, because their path is known, they can plan important components of their lives, which may include paying off college loans, buying a home, getting married, etc. Our system is now stable.

How should our salary schedule relate to the competitive landscape? As we have already eluded, even though the TSORE firm is unique and offers benefits that our competitors do not, we do continue to operate within a marketplace. Therefore, there is actually no 'correct' answer to this question. It comes down to our organization's individual philosophy on the subject of pay and scarcity of talent. We have proven that our programs' value propositions are unique, and there is unquestionably a value of that education. If we intend on acquiring the top talent to our programs, then we equally need to recognize the value of the associates that we admit through remuneration. While we might not have to pay the top compensation in our market, we do need to remain competitive. It is very possible to under-compensate ourselves out of the market for the talent that we want. Of course we believe that our students are the best in the market, and so we should also assume that they are smart enough to do the math. We want them focused on their educations, not weighing their options of leaving our firm for a higher paying competitor.

Bonuses. The second major category in the compensation package is the bonus. If we imagine that the salary tool is designed to bring stability to both employee and the organization, then the bonus is intended to reward and incite certain behaviors and successes. Unlike salary, which is most effective when applied monolithically, the bonus structure is nimble and may take many forms. That said, to reinforce stability, our bonuses should also be applied uniformly and openly. The creation of successful bonus structures also requires forethought and intentionality. For a bonus to have its intended consequence, it must be motivational to the recipient. Which is why we suggest that we apply a litmus test to each of the bonuses that we contemplate.

We have repeatedly described our associates as salesmen, as rockstars, and as 'deal guys.' The fact that they haven't closed any deals yet is of little consequence. We know that in time, they will. However, unlike the partners in our firms who operate on large, performance-based compensation, our younger Associates have neither the perspective nor the patience to wait two to three years for a bonus. And so we must devise ways to reward them for 'mini' successes. These act as periodic adrenaline shots, which they will find quite motivating.

Organization and preparation are the keys to designing a compelling bonus plan. As such, the authors suggest that each intended bonus be addressed using the criteria listed in Figure 11 before implementation.

Litmus Test for Proposed Bonuses

1. What behavior is the bonus intended to reward or illicit?
2. To whom should this bonus apply?
3. How often is the bonus applicable or periodically dispersed?
4. Does the recipient control the outcome for which they are rewarded?
5. What other alternative bonuses should be considered to address this behavior?

Figure 11. Bonus Litmus Test

Of course the litmus test should be written out, debated and accepted by the leadership team.

Reverse bonus. Another issue to consider is that bonuses can be applied multi-directionally. Often when we think of the bonus, we imagine it to be an accrual to our compensation for performing some task with excellence. This is certainly a valid approach, but not applicable to all behaviors that we are attempting to foster. For instance, consider the possibility that something much less tangible such as 'a respect for other people's time' is a key value for our organization. The organization expects each team member to be on time and prepared for every internal and project meeting and decides to implement a punctuality bonus.

It is difficult to positively reward someone for this kind of behavior. Do they accrue a $20 bonus for every meeting for which they arrive properly prepared? Of course this bonus would fail for numerous reasons: it would be unwieldy to manage, it is not of sufficient size to be motivational, and its subjectivity would simply add the chaos to the organization that we are trying to remove. Another option though is a preloaded bonus, which would diminish each time the leader of the meeting designated the attendees to be non-punctual or ill-prepared. Imagine our employees having a quarterly a pre-awarded quarterly bonus of $300 – and each occurrence in which they were not prepared and respectful of the time of the team, they would see $20 deducted from that account. We would quickly witness a culture in which 'on-time' habits would be respected. Think of this as a reverse bonus.

Bonus Types. Regardless of whether it is applied additively or punitively, all bonuses are still not created equal. And while we could come up with a multitude of examples of potential bonuses and structures, they would all fit into three primary buckets: the *performance bonus*, the *project bonus* and the *discretionary bonus*. Within these three, there is not one type that is inherently better or worse than another. The key to their effectiveness is that they are applied intentionally and appropriately to achieve their intended consequence. The key to effectiveness boils down to correctly answering the following questions:

1. How much control does the recipient exert over the outcome for which they are being rewarded?
2. Is the reward significant enough to motivate the individual?
3. How often is the reward distributed?

Clearly, a bonus becomes increasingly influential based on whether the recipient feels significant ownership of its outcome, if the size of the bonus is sizable enough to motivate and if it is distributed regularly. As we mentioned, each of the three bonus buckets serves a different purpose, which are as follows:

The Performance Bonus. Performance bonuses are intended to address behavioral issues. They may be awarded either additively of punitively. Although there are exceptions, typically they are correlated to an individual and not a team. Issues to consider when structuring a performance bonus include:

1. *Size.* As with any bonus, the reward needs to be significant enough that it is motivational to the recipient and reflects a value that the firm feels that it is consequential to the Associate's long-term career performance.
2. *Number.* And while there are likely a plethora of behaviors that are useful to our success, we do not want to lose the significance of a key behavioral bonus amongst a morass of performance bonuses. Therefore we should limit the bonus to issues that are fundamental to a developer's success and

directly aligned with the firm's values. No more than three performance bonuses should be administered simultaneously.

3. *Frequency.* When we structure the distribution of a performance bonus, it is important to pay it out in directly foreseeable installments. Using again the example of the punctuality bonus described earlier, the disbursement should be regular to be effective. Monthly disbursements, similar to a regular commission structure could be highly motivational (especially if it represented a significant percentage of the associate's monthly income); however, quarterly distribution is also very reasonable.

Individuals adjust their behavior when they can see an immediate benefit to doing so. The more distant the bonus, the less real and believable it is. For instance, being unprepared for a team meeting in February is motivationally irrelevant if the consequence is that we will lose $20 in the following December. Whereas, it is highly consequential if it represents a $20 loss in this month's income. Accordingly, annual bonuses are not motivational and not recommended for any performance bonuses.

4. *Definition.* The performance bonus is intended to reward a specific behavior and not a general series of behaviors. We must be specific in how the bonus applies. For instance, the punctuality bonus is very clear and administrable. A 'professional conduct' bonus on the other hand is very muddy. It denotes a series of behaviors and potentially adds a fair

amount of subjectivity, both of which add to the chaos that we are trying to remove from the organization. Note that 'professional conduct' may be an overarching theme to which all of the performance bonuses relate. But remember that we have six years with the associates, and individual performance bonuses may change throughout those years, once a behavior has been sufficiently ingrained in the organization. Once again, simplicity is the key to the performance bonus; if we can't clearly define it, they can't value it.

A final thought on the performance bonus, whether administered additively or punitively, is that its goal is to teach and reward for positive general behaviors. We want each of our associates to earn 100% of that bonus. That means that we are creating a stronger, more stable organization. Their success in receiving as much bonus as possible is a reflection of our mentoring success. If they are consistently only earning 70% of their bonus, then we are not effective teachers. Our success relies on making them successful.

The Project Bonus. One of the maxims within this book is that the purpose of the development firm is to produce exceptional developers. It does however remain the purpose of the project team itself to produce exceptional buildings. The focus on the building and the positive dynamics of the project team are reinforced with the project bonus. Similar to the performance bonus above, there are factors within the way that it is structured, which will determine the project bonuses ultimate success.

1. *Frequency.* Disbursements on a project timeline are typically tied to critical events in the project lifecycle. These may include: land closing, debt closing, substantial completion, lease-up or sell-out. The key consideration when determining which events deserve a bonus disbursement should also be determined using our 'outward focus' strategy, and should be based on events in which the project team has some control.

   For instance, if project financing is handled by a separate finance team, then even though there is a liquidity event for the firm, closing debt is not an event which is controlled by the Associate and the reward would not directly reflect their success. It was the success of the finance team and only the finance team should be bonused at that time. Receipt of building permits might be a better event to reward.

2. *Size.* As we have described, each bonus is a part of the overall compensation package for the associate. These young students consider their entire income when they make their living decisions. From our perspective, we senior developers make much of our compensation based on these critical project events and it is a very logical inclination to heavily weight the associates' bonuses to our milestones. Before going down this path, we need to consider two things:

   a. The senior developers and partners have a considerably greater responsibility in the project's overall success.

   b, The percentage of irregularly recurring bonuses has a much greater impact on those with a smaller base income.

As such, we may find that in their early years the Associates' reward from project milestones should be minimized – although we do need to make sure that their monthly income (salary and performance bonuses) is a reasonable livable sum. After all, we add chaos by keeping an associate financially uncomfortable.

3. *Bonus Alignment.* When it comes to the distribution of the project bonus, there are really two issues at play: preparation and distribution. As far as preparation goes, it is much easier to create a standard bonus matrix that is tied to the Associates and based on their year at the time of distribution. In other words, if permits are received on the associates first day as a 3rd year associate, then they should be compensated as a 3rd year – even though the work led to this event occurred during their work as a 2nd year associate. The key is simplicity. If we leave room for interpretation, then we open the door to unnecessary chaos.

The second issue is distribution. One of the main purposes of the project bonus is to reinforce the importance of the team as a highly-performing unit. The head of that team is a partner and it is that individual who should present the disbursements. Put on a show when distributing a bonus. If we fail to recognize the 'attaboy' factor of the bonus, we get less out of the act.

The Discretionary Bonus. The discretionary bonus is prevalent in our industry and has acquired stigmas, both good and bad. We have all worked with employers who promise discretionary bonuses, and it is not uncommonly used in an attempt to get us to accept a lower base compensation for the promise of some future, greater reward. When used in this form, there are two primary problems:

1. The bonus actually acts as a disincentive; it rewards nothing, elicits no positive behavior, and its ambiguity almost always results in mistrust and a diminished culture.

2. It is offensive in its patriarchal nature. It is a way of treating the recipient like a pigeon, waiting at their employer's feet for some benevolent breadcrumbs.

When Associates of any level are planning their lives they have limited resources. Regardless of whether these are small or great, we all have to make decisions based on our definitive compensation. The discretionary bonus acts as a limit on our ability to create those plans that give us stability outside of the office. Deterring our team's ability to add the necessary stability to their lives invites resentment, and therefore chaos.

On the other hand, when used as a gift, a discretionary bonus can be a wonderful 'thank you' to an employee. A Christmas Bonus for instance, is a great discretionary bonus. But since we as employers can choose to give a discretionary bonus, it should not be considered as part of the associate's compensation package. Unlike the others, discretionary bonuses should not be pre-published nor even discussed at time of hiring. When we discuss a revenue stream, we invite the Associate to have an expectation – one which we may or may not fulfill. That is exactly the sort of ambiguity that we are attempting to remove from the organization.

Toys. There is a subcategory of the discretionary bonus that can be created which can be exceptionally motivating: toys. As we've said so many times, our students are future development rock stars. And rock stars need cool gear. When we provide some of the items that they covet or at least associate with the persons that they are try to become, we remind them that we value their future. Toys can also reinforce for them the ways that we expect them to represent our organizations. This category of discretionary bonus can provide a high-impact result, often for less money than the more expensive bonuses. They can reinforce pride and build deep loyalty.

Some examples of great Toys include:

- The cool smartphone, tablet or laptop.
- Badass sunglasses.
- Their first made–to-measure suit, or a shopping spree.
- An old-fashioned straight-razor shave.
- Teeth whitening.
- Spa day (massage, facial, manicure).
- Anything cool that speaks to your Company values.

The key to the success of the Toy bonus is that it reinforces a bigger picture. It is designed to help them to develop an image or a lifestyle that reinforces the firm values. By providing them with select cool toys, we reinforce their belief that we care about their success, and that as their mentors we are invested in them.

Salary to Bonus Ratio. When we consider the total financial compensation package for an associate, we need to keep in mind a couple of key questions: What is the total value of the recurring monthly income for that position? Is it enough to live on? Does it allow for the reasonable lifestyle expectations of someone of that age and with the work requirements that are placed on them? One thing to remember here is to view it from the typical view of someone their age; a 25 year old will have different needs than a 29 year old. They have no risk in our firm and so they will value stability more highly than the entrepreneurial 'eat what you kill' perspective that we have. The key here is to be reasonable. After all, if the compensation package does not provide the ability for overall life stability, then we again invite chaos and our compensation package efforts have failed.

As far as a ratio or percentage goes, there really is no magic bullet. At least in the early years, we may target the package to a 70% salary / 30% bonuses strategy. This keeps the team very focused on the lessons that are being taught within the program. It also creates a sort of 'report card' effect. But once again, each firm must remain competitive within the market when adapting the compensation package to their own unique values, goals, region and specialty.

Vacations. Regardless of where we live, at least in the United States, the subject of vacation is fairly standardized. Two weeks of vacation is common for most professional jobs in most industries. In some cases, additional vacation is a reward for years of service.

From the authors' perspective, the length of vacation that is offered to associates by an individual firm is irrelevant. Our concerns in this chapter revolve around ways to reduce chaos within the firm. And in truth, there is not a lot of chaos caused by this subject. That said, there are a few simple steps that can help further minimize the effect of vacations on the development firm:

1. Create an annual firm calendar that includes all holidays and any black-out dates which would identify any corporate retreats, mandatory seminars, etc.

2. Require that at least 50% of the vacation time be utilized in a single, monolithic block. The advantage to this sort of requirement is that it provides an annual mandatory break that is of significant length, sufficient to ensure that the associate recharge their batteries from the daily intensity of their education. We recognize that some of that time can be used as daily vacations for special events or long weekends. Also, make them take the vacation. Don't pay it out as a bonus. Getting away from work is as valuable to a young Associate as it is to us.

3. A coordinated annual 'summer break' where the entire organization shuts down is also a great option. It ensures that the entire firm recharges at the same time, thereby providing a sort of 'reset button' for the morale and energy of the firm.

Any delineation of vacation length, scheduling restrictions or standardized rules should of course be addressed in the acceptance package that the Associate signs when being admitted into the program.

Mandatory Sabbatical. An additional tool that is not standard within most firms is the sabbatical. We feel every firm should consider the long-term benefits of requiring a month-long sabbatical for employees (associates and partners) every five years. Our firms thrive on a mixture of creativity and doggedly applied project management, as well as the intensity that is required by our mentorship programs. This can take a lot out of our employees and one month away from the office every sixty months can help ensure the long-term viability of our teams.

Conclusion. As we can see in the second iteration of the chart in Figure 12 (as compared with the chart in Figure 10 above), with a bit of forethought, items that contain potential chaos for the organization can be easily neutralized, or rather stabilized.

The Improved Organization	Stable	Chaotic
Office space	•	
Work hours	•	
IT, Cell phones and support	•	
Pay periods	⋆	
Pay scales	⋆	
Bonus	⋆	
Job title and promotions	⋆	
Vacation	⋆	
Project goals	•	
Special projects		•
Education		•

Figure 12. Stability and Chaos within a TSORE Organization

Much of the discussion has addressed the benefits of stability as it regards the learning environment that we are attempting to facilitate. This, in and of itself, delivers a tremendous benefit to the leadership team. After all, anything that makes our mentoring responsibilities more efficient should also make them more effective.

The strategy is very simple; rethink, realign, standardize and publish. What is left is an unencumbered space that is more conducive to learning, creating and performing.

Chapter 18

"There Will Be Blood"

"It is good to have an end to journey toward; but it is the journey that matters, in the end." – Ernest Hemingway

Over the previous seventeen chapters we have traversed an incredible amount of territory. With a journey that began by simply stating a very observable truth: that the current state of our profession is in a self-imposed decline. Rather than just acknowledging that there are forces at work that are eroding the most sacred parts of our profession, our cities and our legacies, we identified them. We pointed at them and gave them a face and a name. Many of the pressures are external, but some are not.

Regardless of our intentions, the leaders of our profession have allowed it to devolve to this state. But the downward spiral is not outside of our control. Our destiny is not yet written in stone and we can still bend our profession's trajectory. If we continue to ignore the decay, one day we may lose this prerogative – but today, right now, redemption remains within our grasp.

Some may argue that what we describe is just natural evolution. Some may argue that a future where the developer is the lackey to Wall Street whims, where product is made simply because it can be entitled and financed, regardless of appropriateness, is fine. They may call that progress. Some may even argue that being an excellent developer who is concerned with issues outside of the site is just too hard, too complicated. To those folks we say, 'We'll see you in the Thunderdome.'

Our first step, if we intend to fix the profession, is to look inward. We must decide whether we have structured our firms to address the industry in its current form, or the industry itself as we believe that it can and should be. Introspection precipitates change and we must lead by example. If our vision is compelling, the bars that we set for our own firms will eventually become a reflection of the industry itself. But it begins with us and like-minded developers, who recognize a responsibility that is greater than only our personal wealth. We must endeavor to create projects that our firm would be proud to design, to build, to invest in, or own and operate.

We must proudly adopt our litmus test for the future projects we undertake. The authors have proposed the basic test. There may be more criteria, based on the many unique aspects of our firm, but we begin with these:

1. Is the project financially viable?
2. Is the project appropriate for present and future good of the city?
3. Does the scale of the proposed project enhance the city at an urban level?
4. Is this the right location for the proposed project?
5. Can the project be designed to be adaptable to future uses or will it need to be torn down when this use is complete?

If we can competently answer these questions 100% of the time, we will create a revolution that elevates our profession. We will decrease the risk within our firms and better protect the investment of our capital partners. We will make ourselves rich by increasing the quality of people's lives. We will make our cities beautiful and responsive and successful again. We won't overbuild or litter the landscape with spec product.

Of course, the achieving this goal is not so simple. Our firms are not designed to really, truly answer the questions posed in the litmus test. Realigning our industry also means realigning our firms. It will be hard and blood will be spilled. But it is overwhelmingly worth it. The previous chapters have been dedicated to making feasible the daunting task of overhauling the broken machine that is our profession. Accordingly, we have analyzed each of the parts – especially the ones that we take for granted. Increased performance of this machine comes from fixing what is broken within almost every firm. It is not simply a matter of growing our buying new skills and functionality.

The question is then 'how is the TSORE intended to be used?' The truth is that this is only the beginning point. It is the catalyst that makes the changes that we propose more attainable. These concepts and solutions represent a cohesive program that must be taken in its entirety, as the sum is truly greater than the parts. It is not a Chinese menu where we 'pick one from column A and two from column B.' Deciding to be a 'values based' organization, but not living up to those values ourselves, will fail. Creating the goal to produce the best developers, but then not hiring the best talent, will fail. Hiring the best associates but then not methodically training them, will fail.

Robert Frost's poem "The Road Not Taken" famously ends "Two roads diverged in a wood, and I-, I took the one less traveled by, And that has made all the difference." We developers now stand at that same fork and are confronted with the choice to continue down a path that we know so well but will lead to the eventual destruction of our profession, or to take another.

The Soul of Real Estate is not creating a new path. It has always been there – albeit looking increasingly weathered and overgrown. The authors are simply providing machetes and pith helmets so that we all may clear the decay. This book was created to make developments' 'path less traveled' a bit less daunting. So we use it as a starting point of what will become a lifelong journey. We use this text to remember why we entered this profession, or to discover its romance for the first time. We use is as a guide to meld our leadership teams together to a singular vision. And we use this text to create a methodology that guides our conversations and as we organize the plan of attack as we establish our new firms.

In concluding the text and beginning our journey, there are three major takeaways that will guide our actions.

The first is a revised and more comprehensive definition of success: Success to the developer is "to enhance the lives and experiences of the community, while turning a reasonable profit to investors." This defines our responsibility.

The second takeaway is the revised definition of developer: "We become developers when we choose to marry what is inspirational in life with what is best for the public through a nimble use of our developers' toolset. We become a developer for a lifetime, and if we are lucky in the decades that follow, for a few of those moments we transcend 'developer' and become a 'Developer.'

This is who we are.

And lastly, there is the Litmus Test. These initial five questions (restated above), combined with any added by our specific firms, are our religion. Within the context of our professional lives, if we spend 50% of our efforts focusing on endeavors that support these three components, 100% of our professional lives will be more fulfilling. Safe travels.

Appendix A
Vision Package

North Druid Hills Apartments
Visioning and Positioning

INTRODUCTION

The North Druid Hills Apartments (NDH) represents a new and unique opportunity for -------------- and for the Toco Hills Sub-market. Nestled on the periphery of Atlanta's most prominent Hasidic Jewish community and directly on one of the area's most traveled corridors, NDH has both the stability and visibility necessary to become an iconic model of sensitive and sustainable development.

THE VISION

Its 5:30 on Friday evening and you are finally escaping the bustle of your Buckhead day job, and are looking forward to a relaxing evening of good dinner and great conversation with friends that you know you spend too little time with. Tonight the gang chose Decatur for dinner, so it's off to Watershed and afterward, possibly a treat at Chocolate Bar – or if you get your second wind maybe the group will pop over to the Highlands for more drinks and some good 'ol blues music.

As you travel down North Druid Hills Road it occurs to you that you are halfway there and instantly the tension in your neck and fingers begins to release. Just ahead is the big bend in the road and you know that once you reach it you are at Toco Hills, then home free. This time is different, today you see a new building off to your right, one that you could swear you had never seen before, but one that looks like it has always been there. It's a beautiful yet historic-feeling manor sprawled effortlessly along this tumultuously traveled stretch of road. Made of stones and bricks and wood, it looks like it is growing directly and elegantly out of the earth.

After passing this oasis, you find yourself noticing the shopping, the grocery stores, the gym, and yuppie lattes – all of the amenities that you are used to, but in a neighborhood setting.

You begin to think about your life – you're not 23 anymore, why are you still living with a bunch of kids? How much nicer it would be to be in a community of adults? How much more fulfilling would it be to be surrounded by people who shared your values, or at least lived their lives by values? After all, this area is only 10 minutes from work, 10 minutes from Midtown, 10 minutes from Decatur or the Highlands… You think to yourself, 'you know what- I think that I might just be home.'

THE TENANT

As with any apartment community, the product is driven by the tenant. However, when proposing a luxury building, the product that the tenant is buying is all the more critical- it is a lifestyle.

Demographics

✦ The average age of tenants will be between 28 and 40. Many of the tenants will be single professionals (perhaps couples living together), and young married couples without children.

✦ Tenants will be multi- cultural, although white and Jewish residents will be predominant. Homogeneity will be found at an economic and educational level. Most of the tenants at NDH will have, or intend to get, graduate degrees.

✦ Tenants will typically work in professional settings (see Work below) and will be on a path to make well above the average income.

✦ Residents of NDH will be split approximately 55%-60% women / 40%-45% men.

✦ The appearance of status is not important to these tenants. Because many of them are products of Atlanta or other metropolises or their suburbs, the residents of NDH will be drawn to more refined spaces and cultural events.

Values

✦ The primary drivers in the tenant's life will be their careers and their values.

✦ Because many of the tenants are away from home and family (though generally have been established in the area for at least 3 years), they value community. They search for groups of peers to hang out with.

✦ These tenants feel that they are cosmopolitan and have an inclusive view of the community. They define themselves but what they believe, not solely by what they do.

✦ NDH residents view home as a place away from work. They appreciate the sense of respite that comes from a moderate (but not long) distance from work.

Work

✦ Because of their education, the majority of the tenants work as professionals. They are 2nd to 4th year associates at law firms. They are accountants and consultants.

✦ They are in pharmaceutical and health insurance sales.

✦ These tenants work average to long hours and do regularly cook.

Play

✦ NDH tenants will be fairly active, in sports and definitely within the community.

✦ These tenants run, bike, and hike. Many will kayak or rock climb, or any other activity that takes them on a short adventure.

✦ They travel to Destin or Savannah or North Carolina. A few go to Hilton Head.

✦ They belong to a sports club for social, as well as physical benefits.

✦ In the evenings, the tenants go to restaurants and bars at least once a week. They are not a part of any one scene but prefer Decatur, Emory, The Highlands and Buckhead.

✦ They drink premium vodka drinks, beer, and are developing a taste for wine, however they are not oenophiles. At restaurants, they order by the glass and by the bottle. You may not see Berringer in their fridge, but don't be surprised to see a bottle of KJ.

✦ They value tradition over trend, multi-national over strictly American, authentic over flashy.

Vehicles / Travel

✦ NDH tenants prefer foreign vehicles.

They prefer...	but not...
BMW 3 Series	
Audi A4 or Volvo	
Infinity	Lexus
Acura	
Volkswagen or Jeep	Kia, or Saturn
But they really want...	
Mercedes	
Range Rover	Hummer

✦ These residents will often choose a used German over a new Japanese or American vehicle.
✦ While they regularly use high-octane gasoline, because of their age they do not value full-service filling stations.
✦ They expect to have clean and shiny vehicles, but do not clean them themselves.

Restaurants / Clubs

The restaurants that they prefer will have active bar scenes. These tenants look for comfortable and relaxed, and are somewhat budget conscious. They will typically plan to hit only 1 or 2 different places in a single evening.

They prefer...	but not...
Buckhead Life Restaurants, and Fifth Group Restaurants	Here To Serve Restaurants
Sports Bars, Tavern at Phipps	Compound, Fever, or East Andrews
Art Openings and Wine Tastings	
Sushi, Chinese, Ethiopian, Indian	Fudrucker's, Chili's, TGIF's
Jazz and Blues Clubs	Beluga
Tapas and Thai	French Food
One Midtown Kitchen, Rathbun's	Joel, Ritz Buckhead
Floataway Café	Bacchanalia
Souper Jenny	Metro Fresh
Whole Foods and Farmers markets	

THE PRODUCT

Considering everything that is known about the NDH tenant, a key success factor is for the community as a whole to portray that 'vision' of an established community with history and refinement. Because a larger than normal percentage of the residents will be orthodox Jews, this will necessitate a rethinking of typical apartment complex norms, both as regards the space and unit layouts, but also the amenities.

Residential

+ Due to their age group and income, there will be a higher than normal percentage of renters that are attracted to one and two bedroom units. However, a few three bedroom and studio units would be attractive.
+ Penthouse units would not be valuable.
+ These units must live like homes and not like apartments.
+ Closet space will be valued, as well as finish level. Bedrooms can be conservative, but the living space must feel 'big.'
+ Glazing and light will be valued as well.

Space

+ Big and light.
+ Traditional style with larger than typical base and crown moulding.
+ Amenities on the first floor with a cozy feel.

Amenities

+ Rethink traditional amenities and amenity juxtapositions. Amenities must focus on contemplation, study, and quality of life.
+ Maximize the cardio portion of the fitness center.

✦ Blend the community spaces, but have a couple of contemplative areas.

Retail

✦ The retail must first serve the surrounding neighborhood. It is not necessarily a draw for the apartment community.
✦ Other ideal retailers would include a drugstore, daycare, or fast-casual restaurant.
✦ Special attention must be paid to the parking segregation and traffic flow between the residential and retail uses.

CHALLENGES

Sub-market

✦ **Resistance to change.** A simple drive through the abutting neighborhoods will indicate the longevity of the residents. Few homes are for sale, and the ones that have traded were bought from individuals who had lived there for decades. This is partially due to proximity to the local temples and orthodox religious law. The residents will be very active and united and the developer's approach must be respectful and deferential for the project to succeed.

Site

✦ **The design of the community must maximize density while being very sensitive to the scale and feel of the abutting neighborhoods.**
✦ **The building facades and streetscapes must address the varied vehicular travel speeds.** We must remain conscious of the fact that one experiences architecture very differently when traveling at 40 mph, 20 mph, or walking. More often than not, sidewalks along streets where travel exceeds 30 mph are superfluous. In the case of NDH, the main street is walkable. We must make this experience of pedestrian travel inviting.

✦ **Due to the mixed-use components, traffic and parking flow will be critical.** There is a single and possibly separate retail component (potentially with a drive thru), and a fully operational apartment complex occurring in 8+ acre site. Navigating the traffic flow, service flow, resident and visitor flow at both peak and non-peak hours must be well planned out, or the complex will be a mess.

Residential

✦ **We must understand that, with this luxury product, we are not differentiating ourselves by the finishes.** The high-level of finishes is simply expected. It is the architecture and articulation that will differentiate us.

✦ **Comfort and lifestyle is the sell.** As regards the public spaces, our litmus test throughout the process will need to be "Does this decision reinforce the community and values of our residents?" If not, we may need to rethink the idea.

✦ **Separation.** The byproducts of the retail portion of NDH must not infect the residential component. Smells, sounds, retail traffic, etc. must be controlled so as not to denigrate the community enjoyment of the residents.

Retail

✦ **Standard ceiling heights and security issues will be critical to retail tenants.** Pharmacies and banks in particular have very specific tolerances for security that must be taken into account from the initial design stage.

✦ **Signage will play a key role.** The retailer will want very clear signage to drive customers to the site. We must be cognizant to ensure maximum visibility, but not allow signage to detract from the overall community.

+ **Access for deliveries will also be important.** The developer must also have an understanding of the delivery needs of the various retailers as well as controlling schedules and noise associated with servicing the retail portion of the project, so as not to disturb the community.
+ **Venting and grease-traps.** Consideration must be given to any food-service tenant proposed for the retail at NDH. We should avoid restaurant concepts that have a strong fried, barbeque, or fish component, so as not to disturb our tenants' quality of life.

Leasing

+ **The leasing team must be top-notch at NDH.** The average renter will be considerably more sophisticated at this property. A seasoned manager will drive the culture of the staff and a relaxed feel for the outfits of the staff will suffice.

OPPORTUNITIES

Sub-market

+ **Developers have typically ignored the cultural and ethnic needs of this well-established community.** Sensitivity to this diversity will be well received.
+ **Lack of luxury apartment product.** With the conversion of the Post Peachtree building in 2006, there are no true major luxury apartments in Atlanta. There are a few, very nice, very traditional complexes such as Gables Rock Springs that will be direct competition for NDH (although GRS is more geared to Emory students).
+ **The growing single and 'recently coupled' market that desires the location, security and amenities the development will offer.**

Site

✦ **Key visibility.** Due to its nearly 3/10ths of a mile in length, few residential complexes in Atlanta will have the visibility that is inherent at NDH.

✦ **'A refined urban retreat.'** Due to its location and the surrounding nondescript 1950s architecture, we have the opportunity to create a sophisticated and sprawling façade. The aesthetic will be refined but not pretentious.

Residential

✦ **'God is in the details.'** The architecture of NDH must be honest and appropriate. The building must feel 'right.' Structural details can be expressed and faux articulation should be limited only to reinforcing the aesthetic composition.

✦ **Rethinking 'amenity.'** As has been discussed in multiple ways throughout this paper, the juxtaposition of the amenities is important. Amenities cannot be boxes connected only by a corridor, they must interact with each other, yet the sense of 'here' and 'there' must be respected.

Sales / Leasing

✦ **Professional, formal, nice looking.** NDH needs to be staffed with the best of the best. They must be caring and attentive without pretense or formality. Your staff is also your neighbor.

UNIQUE PROPOSITIONS

Sub-market

+ **Connectivity and seclusion.** In addition to being the convenient to Decatur, Midtown and Buckhead, NDH is also a step removed from bustle of these areas. The complex is half a mile from I-85 and Buford Highway.

Site

+ **Walkable location.** It is a 5 minute walk to over 400,000 SQ/FT of retail space at Toco Hills which contains two grocery stores, and LA Fitness and multiple restaurants and amenities.
+ **The luxury to create a special 'place.'** This will be achieved through the design of the pedestrian streetscape and the creative use of street furniture such as street lights, spacious sidewalks, park benches, etc.
+ **Sometimes 'more' is just 'more.'** Simplicity to the outdoor amenity spaces will be preferred over 'kitchy' spaces. The ability to go outside and read a book will be valued over a faux 'zen garden.'

Made in the USA
Lexington, KY
18 June 2014